MYSTICS & MIRACLES

OTHER BOOKS BY BERT GHEZZI

Voices of the Saints: A Year of Readings

The New Jerusalem Bible: Saints Devotional Edition

Getting Free: How to Overcome Persistent Personal Problems

Being Catholic Today: Your Personal Guide

50 Ways to Tap the Power of the Sacraments: How You and Your
Family Can Live Grace-Filled Lives

Guiltless Catholic Parenting from A to Y: Nobody Knows
Everything There Is to Know, but Here's Wisdom to Help You
Do It Well

MYSTICS &

MIRACLES

True Stories of Lives Touched by God

BERT GHEZZI

LOYOLAPRESS.

CHICAGO

LOYOLAPRESS.

3441 N. Ashland Avenue
Chicago, Illinois 60657

Mystics and Miracles is a revised and expanded version of *Miracles of the Saints,* which was published by Zondervan in 1996.

Credits continued on page 189

Featured on the cover are (top row, from left to right) St. Teresa of Ávila, St. Francis of Assisi, St. Elizabeth of Hungary, St. Catherine of Siena, (second row, from left to right) St. Joan of Arc, St. Martin de Porres, St. Perpetua, Bl. Padre Pio, (third row, from left to right) St. Ignatius of Loyola, St. Dominic, St. Francis Xavier, St. Partick.

Interior design by Nick Panos

Library of Congress Cataloging-in-Publication Data

Ghezzi, Bert.
    Mystics and miracles : true stories of lives touched by God / Bert Ghezzi.
      p. cm.
    Includes bibliographical references.
    ISBN 0-8294-1772-9
     1. Christian saints—Biography. 2. Mystics—Biography. 3. Miracles. I. Title.

BX4655.3 .G48 2002
282'.092'2—dc21
  [B]   2001050192

PRINTED IN THE UNITED STATES
02 03 04 05 06 07 08 09 RRD 9 8 7 6 5 4 3 2 1

For William G. Storey

Contents

I tell you the truth, anyone who has faith in me will do what I have been doing. He will do even greater things than these, because I am going to the Father. And I will do whatever you ask in my name, so that the Son may bring glory to the Father.

JOHN 14:12–13

Acknowledgments

Thanks to Donald E. Fishel and John B. Leidy, Jr., my saint-watcher friends, for their many good ideas and suggestions, and to Donald especially for the use of his vast library. I also appreciate my editors: Ann Spangler, who made this a better book by making me rewrite it; Jim Manney and Heidi Hill, who made it even better with their expert refinements. I am indebted to my friend and agent, Joseph Durepos, for his ebullient inspiration, encouragement, and assistance. Thanks, too, to Fr. George Lane, S.J., Terry Locke, and everyone at Loyola Press for their enthusiastic and energetic publication of *Mystics and Miracles.* Most of all, thanks to my good and long-suffering wife, Mary Lou, who will surely become a saint for having put up with me.

Introduction

Miracles intrigue us. They burst into our humdrum routines with startling revelations of the supernatural realm. Some people dismiss them as imagined or psychosomatically induced phenomena. But most of us welcome news of visions, healings, and other divine interventions. We long for a taste of the supernatural and value new evidence that there is more to life than we can see and touch and feel. Wouldn't each of us love to experience a miracle? A personal miracle would comfort us, demonstrating that God cares enough to touch our lives.

Mystics are men and women who can offer us the evidence we desire. They are wonder-workers who have fulfilled Jesus' prediction that his disciples would perform greater works than he did. Their miracles fascinate us because they are windows to the supernatural. But more than that, mystics show us what can happen when God touches human beings. Their lives paint a picture of what men and women become when God transforms them.

We get the word *mystic* from a Greek root that means "mystery." A mystic is a person who is "introduced into the mysteries." Broadly speaking, all Christians are mystics. We believe that by faith we are initiated into the mysteries of Christ's death and resurrection. But most Christians are not mystics in the technical sense because we have yet to penetrate the Christian mysteries in depth. That's what sets a true mystic apart from the crowd.

Mystics enjoy a special closeness to God. They get rid of all the clutter in their hearts to make more room for God. Often they practice severe self-discipline so they can replace their fleshly desires with longings for God alone. As a way of interceding for Christ's intentions, Lutgarde of Aywières fasted for forty years on bread and a nonalcoholic malt beverage. Dominic imitated Christ, who had no place to lay his head, by sleeping alongside the road with a rock for his pillow. Twenty-first-century Christians are not likely to adopt such

xi

penances, but mystics believe that undertaking these severities helps them draw closer to God.

Mystics frequently experience miraculous phenomena and exercise extraordinary powers. They seem to lapse freely into ecstasy and have been observed at prayer in suspended animation, sometimes for hours. Catherine of Siena went limp in ecstasy at will. Friends reported that they saw Lutgarde of Aywières "float" off the ground. When Anthony of Egypt prayed, he seemed to glow with preternatural radiance. Martin de Porres passed through locked doors. Visions guided Ignatius of Loyola step-by-step in founding the Jesuits. John Bosco visited people in their dreams. Padre Pio appeared in two places at the same time. The list could go on indefinitely.

You might think that mystics are so absorbed with God that they can do nothing but worship him. The mystics of the past prayed for long stretches, but they were also activists. Saints like Catherine, Martin, and Elizabeth of Hungary exhausted themselves in service all day long. Then they prayed most of the night. So as not to disturb her sleeping husband, Elizabeth asked her maid to quietly awaken her for night vigils. During the day she tended the sick in hospitals that she had built for the poor. Solanus Casey counseled and prayed for people twelve hours a day. At night he prayed before the Blessed Sacrament, subsisting on a few hours sleep. Anthony prayed all the time, yet he was very busy. His community-building activities in the desert preserved the Christian ideal for the church of his time, and we still feel the influence of his achievements.

You have probably noticed that most of the mystics I have mentioned so far are saints. All the mystics that I have included in this book are saints or are in the process of being recognized as saints by the Catholic Church. However, many holy women and men are mystics whom the church will never formally acknowledge as saints. Perhaps some have an impediment that prevents their canonization. However, I think most are pray-ers known to God alone, who shun human adulation and keep themselves obscure.

Similarly, all saints are not mystics. All canonized saints were people of prayer who enjoyed an intimate relationship with God. But for a variety of reasons, not all ascended to mystical heights. For example, some were martyred, and others died young before they had an opportunity to advance in union with God.

Over the past several years I have spent every day with the mystics. For the most part, I have enjoyed being with them. Now and then, however, their extremism has made me uncomfortable. Anthony's penances in the desert, for instance, are alien to me. I can't even tolerate sand between my toes when I'm sunning at the beach. The lifelong fasts of Vincent Ferrer and Francis of Paola are not for me. I am unable to go for many hours between meals without snacking. I was so distressed by the self-mutilations of Rose of Lima and Margaret of Cortona that I decided not to write about them. When Rose was praised for her lovely skin, she damaged it with lye. And out of a misguided sense of guilt over past sexual sins, Margaret carved scars into her beautiful face. In my view such actions have little to do with holiness.

xiii

But I feel right at home when the mystics let me see their humanity.

I won't soon forget how Teresa of Ávila has delighted me. I will forever picture her scarfing down a partridge to the shock of a friend who thought she should be fasting. I will also think of her stifling a laugh while a priest denounced her from the pulpit. Francis of Assisi, who sometimes seems so otherworldly, has also endeared himself to me. On his deathbed he asked for marzipan, his favorite treat. He had just told one of his brothers to ask Jacoba, a longtime friend and noblewoman of Rome, to bring him some when she came to the door with a tray of the dessert. In a charming display of humanness, Francis bent the rule that forbade women to enter a friar's room. He instructed that the woman be called "brother" so that she could approach his bed and serve him the marzipan.

As an inveterate practical joker myself, I cherish the high jinks of John Bosco. When two friends schemed to have him confined to an insane asylum, he had *them* locked up instead. I love the way Elizabeth of Hungary once dealt with a fourteen-year-old boy. She confronted him about the way he dressed. Then, at his request, she prayed for him until he was overcome by God's presence. Where can I sign my teen up for that kind of treatment?

I have received great encouragement from St. Patrick. When he was about fifty, he once offhandedly admitted that his youthful fervor was gone and he felt spiritually tepid. My own enthusiasm seems to have lost some of its zip, so Patrick's frankness gives me a boost.

It's no surprise that most mystics appear to ignore the marvels that swarm about them. They give God exclusive credit for miracles he accomplishes through them. Only a few mystics of the past seemed to deliberately work signs and wonders. These were the full-scale miracle workers such as Francis of Paola, Vincent Ferrer, and John Bosco.

Some mystics even seem annoyed by their miracles. Lutgarde begged God to take back her gift of healing because long lines of petitioners kept her from prayer. Martin tried to hide his healing gifts by pretending to use compresses, herbs, and other medicines. Anthony claimed to have no miraculous powers, but when he sent people away, they always discovered that their prayers had been answered. Francis of Assisi had to be persuaded to pray for the sick because he felt unworthy of any miracle. And the feisty teetotaler Catherine of Siena was once so embarrassed by the miraculous appearance of a medicinal wine in her behalf that she told Christ to undo the wonder. "Who asked you for this miracle anyway?" she cried, with just a pinch of defiance.

Why are the mystics' lives marked by so many miracles? Why do they experience so many visions, healings, and other supernatural events? I have some thoughts on that question.

First, mystics are lovers. They love God with their whole heart and soul, and they love people with every ounce of their being. When they put their love into action, signs and wonders flow. Out of pure affection, Theresa Margaret sympathetically kissed an ailing friend, who was instantly healed by that little gesture. Anthony of Padua lovingly breathed a prayer over a troubled young man, who was instantly relieved and transformed. Love moved Perpetua and her companions in prison to pray for Felicity, who gave safe birth to her daughter one month prematurely.

Do I need to list more examples? I could go on for a long time. Scripture says that "God is love" and that "God has poured out his love into our hearts" (see 1 John 4:16 and Romans 5:5). I believe that love causes, or at least occasions, miracles because God is in it.

Second, if you look at it from another angle, you could say that mystics do not work miracles at all. You could argue that not even those who produce the greatest miracles are actually wonder-workers. They just draw near and stay close to Christ, who is the real miracle worker. The mystics are intimate friends of Jesus, and their personal relationship with him is so secure that they can ask him for favors and expect to receive them. Once, for example, Catherine of Siena teased Raymond of Capua by pretending that she couldn't obtain a healing for their friend who was deathly ill. When Raymond asked Catherine why she let the man lie dying, she said, "What? Do you think I am God that I can deliver someone from death?"

"Don't give me that!" said Raymond. "I know that Jesus does whatever you ask him to." Of course, Catherine had already asked, and Jesus had already healed their friend.

Third, God grants the mystics a foretaste of heaven and allows the supernatural realm to penetrate their earthly lives. For brief periods their humanity appears to take on divine qualities. Catherine of Siena taught that all the way to heaven is heaven because Christ said

"I am the way." Heaven has come down to earth. Supernatural reality is so present in the mystics that it cannot be contained in these mere earthen vessels. It breaks out in ecstasies and other miraculous phenomena.

Finally, many mystics devote themselves to Christ in his greatest miracle—the cross. The mystery of Jesus' death and resurrection consumed Francis of Assisi, Gertrude the Great, Teresa of Ávila, Padre Pio, and many others. When the mystics invoke the power of the cross, wonders occur. Clare of Assisi once walked into an infirmary, made the sign of the cross five times, and five sick sisters immediately got out of bed—healed. In the name of Christ crucified, Clare also stopped an army that was poised to attack her convent; Dominic restored to life a young man who had died in a fall from his horse; and Vincent Ferrer worked at least three thousand wonders. The mystics' devotion to the cross of Christ overflows in miracles.

Those are my thoughts on the subject. Let's see what you think after you read about mystics and their miracles.

PART ONE

MIRACLES *of* LOVE

The saints differ from us in their exuberance, the excess of our human talents. Moderation is not their secret. It is in the wildness of their dreams, the desperate vitality of their ambitions, that they stand apart from ordinary people of good will.

PHYLLIS McGINLEY

od gave us mystics to show us that ordinary people can live extraordinary lives. He never meant for us to put them on pedestals or view them as superhuman, far beyond anything we mortals could ever hope to be. Mystics are not preternaturally gifted aliens from another planet, but human beings just like us. We esteem them not because, like Superman, they have supernatural powers and can leap tall buildings in a single bound, but because they show us how to live good lives.

When I look closely at mystics, I wonder if I grasp what it means to really imitate them. They did everything in extremes. No cost seemed too high. Me, I'm much more balanced. I count the cost all right, but I often find the price is steeper than I'm willing to pay.

St. Theresa Margaret was ill herself but put aside her own suffering to care for the sick sisters in her convent. I'm not that way. If I get sick, I hop into bed and expect someone to wait on me.

Solanus Casey humbly accepted decisions of his superiors that severely restricted his life and ministry. For half a century he labored without complaint. I'm not like him. Even little inconveniences chafe me. I fight back, big time—just ask the clerks in our local stores.

What can I say about St. Elizabeth of Hungary, who though a queen spent herself and her fortunes serving Christ in the poor? Or St. Martin de Porres? For fifty years he lived every moment of each day for God and for others.

When I stand myself beside these giants, I feel puny.

Comedian Stephen Wright says he once went to a convenience store that bragged it was open twenty-four hours, only to find it closed. Later, the proprietor explained that his store *was* open twenty-four hours, just not twenty-four hours in a row! That's how I am in my imitation of the saints. I'm inconsistent. I try to be like the saints. But only in some ways. And not all of the time.

However, I keep looking at them. I try to stay close to them. I think that if I draw nearer to them, they might infect me with their virtue.

Healing Touch
St. Martin de Porres (1579–1639)

Virtue is our Everest, and those who climb highest are most worth admiring.

PHYLLIS MCGINLEY

Martin de Porres was a forerunner of modern social activists. Consider the remarkable record of his achievements at Holy Rosary Monastery in Lima, Peru, most of which he completed in addition to his routine tasks. Just reviewing his generosity may make us hyperventilate with exhaustion.

Martin single-handedly transformed his monastery into a service center, distributing food and clothing daily to hundreds of people. He also made it a prototype of a modern clinic by inviting the sick to come there to have their diseases cured. And they came in droves. Martin raised vast sums of money that he gave to the poor. Once, he provided dowries for twenty-seven impoverished girls, who would have been unable to marry otherwise. He loved the homeless children of Lima, and for these waifs he planned, funded, and built an orphanage and a school. He arranged for the best possible staff, sparing nothing to hire the most qualified caregivers and teachers.

He accomplished all of this out of his own extreme poverty. He possessed only one shabby tunic, yet he supplied comfort and help for thousands over a period of nearly fifty years. That's the real miracle in his life.

5

Martin was born in Lima, Peru, on December 9, 1579. Less than fifty years before, Francisco Pizarro and his conquistadors had seized the vast Peruvian empire of the Incas. In their rapacious pursuit of gold and power, the Spaniards cruelly destroyed the lives of the native people. Martin himself was a child of the conquest: he was the natural son of John de Porres, a conquistador, and Anna Velázquez, a free black woman. During Martin's lifetime, Peru was just beginning to recover from the Spanish invasions.

When Martin was twelve years old, his mother apprenticed him to a barber-surgeon, who trained him in the medical practices of the day. The youth became a medical expert, mastering the healing skills he would use to serve others for the rest of his life. At that time, Martin also apprenticed himself to Christ. The youthful disciple spent long periods in prayer every night. Often he was so rapt in contemplation that he seemed to lose contact with the world around him.

Martin used herbal medicines, poultices, and other natural remedies to heal the sick, but eventually he discovered that he possessed supernatural gifts of knowledge and healing. Sometimes miracles happened directly through Martin's prayer or touch. However, he worried that his supernatural gifts might draw undue attention to him and cause him to become proud, so he always tried to hide them by pretending to use some herb or other medicine.

Once, Martin visited a woman whom doctors had diagnosed with a life-threatening hemorrhage. The poor lady was so upset with anxiety that Martin had to assure her repeatedly that she would not bleed to death. When he prayed for her, the Lord revealed to him that she would recover. Then, in a feeble effort to conceal his miraculous powers, he gave the sick woman an apple and told her to eat it. As he predicted, in a few days she had returned to perfect health.

In 1594, at age fifteen, Martin became a lay helper of the Friars Preachers at the monastery of the Holy Rosary in Lima. Nine years later Martin entered the Dominican order by professing the vows of a religious brother.

Martin possessed such astonishing healing gifts that I must resist the temptation to recount the story of his life in great detail. But two miracles in particular reveal something of his remarkable character and gifts.

Little did Francis Velasco suspect how difficult it would be to leave the monastery of the Holy Rosary once he had entered it as a novice. Barely a month had passed when his father arrived to woo him away with the promise of riches and power. The senior Velasco had risen to a high rank in the Spanish government. In fact, the Spanish king had authorized him to pass on his former post as secretary of the treasury to his son, Francis. The young man found this offer too alluring to resist. Afraid to face his superiors, Francis decided instead to steal away with his father at midnight. But just as he was about to slip away, a surprise visitor startled him. It seems that Martin de Porres had been praying when suddenly he sensed the need to find Francis and comfort him.

Never one to mince words, Martin accosted the young man. "Are you going to abandon the house of God for the office of the secretary of the treasury? It is better to serve God than to live in your father's house. Believe me, what you were unwilling to do out of love for God, you will do out of fear of God."

Martin's strange knowledge must have frightened the youth, for he decided to remain in the monastery that night. A few hours later, Francis came down with a high fever. Once he had recovered, neither the midnight warning nor the illness was enough to convince him of his calling. He tried two more times to depart, each time becoming seriously ill.

The third and final time, Francis's illness was so severe that a physician by the name of Dr. Cisneto declared him a hopeless case. The doctor ordered him confined to his bed, where his fever soared and his pleural cavities swelled with fluid. There seemed little hope of his recovery.

Then, one night, despite locked doors to both the building and the room, Martin de Porres stood beside the sick man's bed. In his hands he held an old brass brazier filled with glowing coals, a branch of rosemary, and a clean tunic. Martin dropped the rosemary on the coals, and the room filled with a blue, aromatic smoke. Then he helped Francis to his feet and wrapped him in a blanket.

Martin proceeded to turn the mattress, change the sheets, and sponge Francis's fevered body, finally covering it with the fresh tunic. Thus tenderly cared for, the youth stared at Martin and asked whether he would die.

"Do you want to die?" Martin asked.

"No," he said.

"Then you will not die."

"But how did you enter the room when both doors were locked?"

"My boy," said Martin, "who told you to meddle in such things?" Then he departed as swiftly and mysteriously as he had arrived.

Francis slept soundly. When he awakened in the morning, all of his symptoms were gone. Dr. Cisneto, in his amazement, proclaimed it a miracle. Because of Martin's patient intervention, Francis Velasco continued in his vocation as a Dominican.

Martin made many such unexplained night visits to the sick, according to the testimony of his brothers at the monastery. He always seemed to appear on the other side of locked doors with an armload of healing paraphernalia.

On another occasion, Felician de Vega fell deathly ill while traveling through Lima, en route to take up his office as archbishop of Mexico. He suffered from a fever and a severe, persistent pain on the side of his chest. All the doctors' remedies had failed to cure him. De Vega had heard about Martin's healing gifts, for despite all the pretenses Martin had used to disguise them, he had become famous. Desperate for relief, the archbishop demanded that Martin come immediately to his bedside.

Martin's superior ordered him to go in haste, so he had no time to gather his medicines. He worried that he had no decoys to distract attention from his miraculous powers, but he had no choice. He had to obey. As soon as Martin arrived, the archbishop commanded him to stretch out his hand.

"But what would a prelate like Your Excellency want with the hand of a poor black man?" asked Martin. He knew what was coming.

"Didn't the father provincial tell you to do whatever I said?"

"Yes, my lord."

"Then put your hand here."

Marvelously, when Martin gently touched the archbishop's side, the pain evaporated. Martin tried to pull back his hand. "Isn't that enough, my lord?"

"Leave it where it is," commanded the archbishop, and he pressed Martin's hand more tightly against his body. As he did, the fever and all discomfort vanished. Now altogether cured during this brief visit, de Vega unceremoniously sent Martin back to the monastery.

Embarrassed that he had been compelled to display his gift, Martin returned to Holy Rosary determined to quell any temptation to pride. He grabbed a broom and began to sweep randomly and then found some toilets to clean.

"Brother Martin," asked one of the priests, "wouldn't you be better off in the palace of the archbishop of Mexico?"

Paraphrasing Psalm 84, Martin replied, "'I have chosen to be a slave in the house of my God.' Father, I think one moment spent in doing what I am doing right now is more important than many days spent in the house of the Lord Archbishop."

9

Martin did not spend much time thinking about miracles. They were God's business, not his. He spent his daylight hours indefatigably caring for others, especially Lima's poor. He devoted his nights to prayer and penance. He slept only sporadically and as little as possible, usually on a hard bench in a room near the infirmary.

Martin knew 1 Corinthians 13 by heart: "If I have a faith that can move mountains, but have not love, I am nothing. . . . [Love] always protects, always trusts, always hopes, always perseveres." The profound charity described in that text shaped his life: he strove to make everyone around him comfortable but ignored his own discomfort.

He fed the hungry poor, nourishing their bodies with food and their souls with good counsel.

Martin regularly brought Lima's sick and infirm into the monastery to care for them, often in his own room. When some brothers complained, he found places for the sick at his sister's home nearby. He was frequently ill himself with malarial fever, but he paid no attention to it.

As the one in charge of the monastery's wardrobe, Martin kept his brothers properly dressed but also generously clothed the poor. The hungry always knew that Martin would feed them. At suppertime he would scavenge in the dining hall for food to serve the blacks, Indians, and Spaniards who crowded outside the door. Often he gave away his own meals. At times when food was in short supply, it seemed to multiply as Martin dispensed it.

The thought of Martin de Porres makes me confront my own self-indulgence. My personal concerns seem to gobble up most of my money. Oh, I have had flashes of generosity in which I have mailed a check to a philanthropic organization. Rarely have I reached out personally to the poor. Now, I don't live lavishly, I tell myself, but I do see to it that I am well fed and comfortable. Perhaps imitating Martin de Porres, even in some small way, will chip away at my selfishness. It may take a miracle to move that mountain. But I will try.

Love's Charter

If I speak in the tongues of men and of angels, but have not love, I am only a resounding gong or a clanging cymbal. If I have the gift of prophecy and can fathom all mysteries and all knowledge, and if I have a faith that can move mountains, but have not love, I am nothing. If I give all I possess to the poor and surrender my body to the flames, but have not love, I gain nothing.

Love is patient, love is kind. It does not envy, it does not boast, it is not proud. It is not rude, it is not self-seeking, it is not easily angered, it keeps no record of wrongs. Love does not delight in evil but rejoices with the truth. It always protects, always trusts, always hopes, always perseveres.

1 Corinthians 13:1–7

Little Miracles of Affection
St. Theresa Margaret (1747–70)

Be devoted to one another in brotherly love. Honor one another above yourselves. Never be lacking in zeal, but keep your spiritual fervor, serving the Lord. Be joyful in hope, patient in affliction, faithful in prayer.

ROMANS 12:10–12

Anna Maria Redi was a lover. She made everyone around her feel valuable. If you had visited her, she would have made you the center of attention. She would have seen to it that you were comfortable, served you something to eat or drink, and then barraged you with questions about your life. "Now, tell me all about you," she would say. Anna Maria's smiling eyes would hold you fixed in her gaze, and she would celebrate everything you told her. You would have to tear yourself away from this charming young woman. And she would leave you with an exhilarating sense of approval.

Anna Maria showered this kind of affection on the nuns of St. Theresa's Convent in Florence, Italy, which she entered at age seventeen. As Sister Theresa Margaret of the Sacred Heart, she regaled her sisters with personal kindnesses, which they enjoyed especially when they were sick. Her tender words and care touched them all. The elderly sisters of the cloister in particular were delighted with Theresa Margaret. She brought a gentle relief to their lives, which had been hardened by the rigors of the Carmelite rule. Her idealism stirred them to rekindle their own, and they sensed in her a promise of refreshment.

Theresa Margaret's affection for her companions occasioned numerous little miracles. She was especially close to Mother Theresa Adelaide, an elderly woman who was stone deaf. Illness confined Theresa Adelaide to the infirmary, where the two friends, like a fading grandmother and a sprightly granddaughter, were often absorbed

11

in conversations. These remarkable visits astounded observers because Theresa Adelaide could not hear a single word that others spoke, but she had no difficulty hearing Theresa Margaret.

The sisters also noticed another little miracle. When Theresa Adelaide lay dying, she would whisper Theresa Margaret's name. The young sister would come flying from far ends of the convent, where the sound of her friend's voice could not possibly have reached her.

Though Theresa Margaret was a stickler for the cloister's rule of life, on at least one occasion she put her love for a sister above her obedience to the letter of the law. That charitable gesture resulted in a life-changing healing.

Sister Mary Victoria, one of the novices at St. Theresa's, was tormented by a chronic toothache. The affliction was so serious that the superiors wondered whether they should even accept her into the convent on a permanent basis. One day during a meal, Mary Victoria was quivering with pain, and Theresa Margaret, moved by pity, leaned over and kissed her on the cheek. Immediately, Mary Victoria was free of the pain that plagued her. The toothache never recurred, and the young woman became a regular member of the community. The Carmelite rule forbade one sister to kiss another, but Theresa Margaret wasn't thinking about rules that day. She was thinking about love, and that led to a small gesture of kindness, and that led to a miracle.

Theresa Margaret died on March 7, 1770. For fifteen days her body lay exposed without any sign of decomposition. This miracle attracted thousands, who streamed to the convent from Florence and neighboring towns. One day the convent carpenter took a violet from Theresa Margaret's bier and touched it to the face of a woman, who was then instantly healed of a disfiguring skin disease. Another workman took a flower and touched it to his son's arms. The boy was healed of a disease that had crippled him with inflamed joints.

Theresa Margaret's affection seems to have lingered after her death. Her miracles ignited a spiritual renewal in the churches of Florence and of neighboring towns.

St. Theresa Margaret's body has remained incorrupt into the twenty-first century, showing none of the usual signs of decay. You may wonder, as I do, why such things happen. When God allows something that seems to break the laws of nature, he must have a reason for it. Maybe he is telling us something. Something simple like, Look at this woman and love as she did. If you do, you may see miracles happen.

Genuine Love

I desire to love you, O my God, with a love that is patient, with a love that abandons itself wholly to you, with a love that acts, and most important of all, with a love that perseveres.

Just as one who loves a creature thinks of it often, so let the lover of God have him often in his thoughts.

The mirror into which we must look in order to attain divine love is Jesus Christ.

If the actions of our neighbors had a hundred sides, we ought to look at them on the best side.

When an action is blameworthy, we should strive to see the good intentions back of it.

Let us do everything for love and, remembering that love longs for love alone, nothing can appear hard to us.

St. Theresa Margaret

13

Royal Miracles

ST. ELIZABETH OF HUNGARY (1207–31)

Is not this the kind of fasting I have chosen:
to loose the chains of injustice . . .
to set the oppressed free . . . ?
Is it not to share your food with the hungry
    and to provide the poor wanderer with shelter . . . ?
Then your light will break forth like the dawn,
    and your healing will quickly appear;
then your righteousness will go before you,
    and the glory of the LORD will be your rear guard.

ISAIAH 58:6–8

Elizabeth of Hungary was a wife, a mother, an activist, a mystic, and a miracle worker. In her short life, she accomplished far more than most of us ever do, and she did it amid stressful hardships.

Elizabeth was the daughter of King Andrew II of Hungary and his queen, Gertrude. When she was a child, her parents betrothed her to Ludwig, the son of Hermann, the count of Thuringia. At age four, she was sent to Wartburg Castle to be reared with her future husband.

Ludwig grew fond of Elizabeth and eventually fell in love with her. When the young man returned from his travels, he would bring his betrothed little gifts—a rosary, a purse, or gloves. She would run out to meet him, and he would take her on his arm and give her the present.

When Elizabeth was fourteen and Ludwig was twenty-one, he succeeded his father as the count of Thuringia. Against the advice of his counselors, who resented Elizabeth's generosity to the poor, Ludwig married his beloved princess. "I would rather cast away a mountain of gold," he said, "than give her up." Over the next six years, the happy couple had three children.

Ludwig regarded Elizabeth as his special pearl, and he encouraged her pursuit of holiness. Elizabeth instructed her handmaids to awaken her for prayer during the night without disturbing Ludwig. Once, a maid thought she was gently shaking her mistress, only to find that she had taken hold of Ludwig's foot. The frightened young lady explained herself, and Ludwig, perhaps with a sleepy smile, let it pass.

Courtiers regularly criticized Elizabeth for her generous giving to the poor. In 1225, Thuringia suffered a grievous famine. To provide for those who were suffering, Elizabeth exhausted her own financial resources and her grain supply. But when household officers complained to Ludwig, he brushed them off.

"Has she disposed of any of my lands?" he asked.

"No," answered her critics.

"Then you have no complaint," he said. "As for her charities, they will bring us God's blessing."

Once, Elizabeth put a leper in the bed that she and her husband shared. Not surprisingly, Ludwig was enraged. He ran into the room and pulled back the blankets. Instead of seeing a leper, however, the count had a vision of the crucified Christ lying on the bed. From then on, he let his wife freely pursue her service to the poor and the sick.

15

With Ludwig's approval, Elizabeth constructed a hospital. To make it accessible to the poor, she located it at the base of the rock atop which the unapproachable castle stood. Elizabeth visited the hospital twice daily so that she could personally minister to the sick. She also fed nine hundred people every day at the castle, in addition to providing for large numbers of the hungry throughout Thuringia. To encourage responsibility among those she served, she gave them opportunities to work in exchange for aid.

PRAYER IN ACTION
St. Cyprian of Carthage (c. 200–58)

The Lord taught us to pray not only in words, but also in actions. He prayed frequently himself and showed us by example what we must do. As Scripture says: "Rising very early in the morning, he left and went to a deserted place, where he prayed" [see Mark 1:35]. But if the sinless one prayed, how much more ought sinners to pray.

When we stand praying, we ought to be watchful and earnest with our whole heart, intent on our prayers. Let all carnal and worldly thoughts pass away. Don't let the soul think on anything except the object of its prayer. Thus the priest prepares the minds of the people by saying, "Lift up your hearts," so that upon the people's response, "We have lifted them up to the Lord," he may be reminded himself to think of nothing but the Lord.

Moreover, those who pray should not come to the Lord with fruitless or naked prayers. Petition is ineffectual when it is a barren entreaty that implores God. For as every tree that bears no fruit is cut down and cast into the fire, so also assuredly words that do not bear fruit cannot deserve anything of God because they are not fruitful in any good action. Thus Holy Scripture instructs us, saying, "Prayer is good with fasting and almsgiving." For he who will reward us on judgment day for our works and alms will even in this life listen mercifully to those who come to him in prayer combined with good works.

One morning Elizabeth found a deformed boy lying on the hospital's threshold. The child was deaf and dumb and so disabled that he could barely drag himself along the ground. His mother had left him at the door, hoping that Elizabeth could help him.

Elizabeth did not know of the child's impairments and tried to speak with him.

"Dear child, who brought you here?" she asked.

No answer.

"From what are you suffering? Will you not answer me?"

Again, no response.

She took pity on the boy, thinking that some demon was at the root of his ailments. "In the name of our Lord," she said loudly, "I command you, and him that is in you, to reply and to tell me where you came from!"

At that, the boy stood up, completely restored to health. Even though he had never spoken before, he could now explain his situation—how his mother had brought him to the hospital and that he had been deaf, dumb, feeble, and deformed from birth. The countess asked him to keep her role in his healing a little secret between the two of them, but he told his mother, and she told everyone she could. So Elizabeth's gift of healing became widely known, and many came seeking her gracious touch.

On another occasion, when Elizabeth was praying at a church near the hospital, she saw a blind man feeling his way about the building. She watched as he slowly moved his hands over the face of a statue of Mary and smiled fondly in recognition.

"Why are you wandering around the church?" she asked.

"I came to find the lady who helps the poor," he said. "First, I came to pray in the church. Now I am going around to feel how long and wide it is."

"Would you like to see the church?" she asked.

"God willing," he said. "But I was born blind."

"Maybe it's best you were blind," said Elizabeth. "You might have fallen into something worse."

"Oh, no," he said. "I would have been glad to work, like everybody else."

"Pray that God will give you light," she said, "and I will pray for you." She knelt nearby and prayed, and as she did, the man received his sight. The two of them celebrated by taking a tour of the church.

In 1227, Ludwig and his army joined a crusade to the Holy Land. He got as far as Otranto, in southern Italy, where he contracted the plague and died. Elizabeth had just given birth to her third child, a daughter, when the news reached Thuringia. At the age of twenty, she had become a widow. In her grief, she is said to have shrieked like a madwoman and run wildly about the castle. "The world is dead to me," she cried, "and all that was joyous in the world."

Grief and turmoil disrupted the last years of Elizabeth's life. Though the facts are unclear, it seems that her husband's relatives forced her from her home. At the same time, she was receiving spiritual direction from Master Konrad of Marburg, a mean-spirited priest who strove to break her will in order to foster her sanctity. He even forced her to send away the maids who had served her all her life, depriving her of the intimate friends she loved the most.

Despite her bitter losses, the young countess endured. She joined the Third Order of St. Francis, the association of laypeople who patterned their lives on his rule. Then she built herself a little house in Marburg, where she lived austerely and continued her ministry to the needy. To earn money for her charity, she fished in the streams, carded wool, and spun cloth. Increasingly, she gave herself over to prayer.

Elizabeth prayed for many hours at a time in church. However, she especially liked to pray in the fields. She cherished her times of meditation near a clear fountain at the foot of a rugged hill. It is said that she even prayed there through driving rain without getting wet.

Elizabeth frequently prayed for others to experience God. Once, she spoke with Berthold, a boy of fourteen, about his extravagant dress.

"Do you think the Savior would have dressed in suede as you do?" she asked.

The youth dodged the question. "Dear lady," he said, "why don't you just pray for me? Maybe I'd change and want to serve God."

"Do you really want me to pray for you?" asked Elizabeth.

"Yes, I do," said Berthold.

Young Berthold seems to have gotten more than he bargained for. As Elizabeth prayed, something extraordinary happened. "Stop, ma'am!" he cried. "I can't stand it any longer! My body is all inflamed!" But she kept on praying until he said he thought his heart would break. Afterward, the young man's behavior revealed that the experience had indeed had a significant spiritual effect on him. Ultimately, he became a member of the Friars Minor, the religious order of St. Francis of Assisi.

Over the years, Elizabeth progressed in mystical prayer. Frequently, she appeared to lose consciousness for long periods. These deep prayer times strengthened her body, and after she emerged from them, she had no need of food. When asked to express how she felt in her ecstasy, she could only respond with words reminiscent of the Song of Songs: "My soul fainted away when my beloved spoke to me."

The mystic lived only two years at Marburg before her health declined. At dawn on November 17, 1231, Elizabeth spoke softly to her attendant, "It is now the time of day when the Lord rose from the grave and broke the doors of hell, and he will release me." The countess died that evening at twenty-four years of age.

The Protectress of the Poor

Acting as a true child of the Gospel, Elizabeth saw in the person of her neighbor the divine Jesus, the only object of her affection. She loved him with so admirable a charity that her delight was to see herself surrounded by the poor, to live and converse with them. She most dearly cherished those whose misery and disgusting maladies rendered them most horrible, and whose appearance would be sufficient to terrify the strongest hearts in the world. She so charitably distributed all her wealth among them that she left herself poor and indigent to supply all things necessary for them in abundance. She was but of that youthful age when children still require instructors, and already she was the good mother, the guardian and protectress of the poor, and her heart was full of compassion for their sufferings.

Pope Gregory IX

Miracles from Failures
VENERABLE SOLANUS CASEY (1870–1957)

For whoever exalts himself will be humbled, and whoever humbles him-self will be exalted.

MATTHEW 23:12

Solanus Casey may well be the most humble person you will meet in these pages.

Perhaps when we are dealing with saints, *humble* ceases to be a comparative adjective. When a person always takes the lowest place, who can be lower? When a person makes him- or herself the servant of all, who can compete? By definition, saints are superlatively humble.

The outline of Solanus Casey's life traces the pattern of biblical humility. From childhood to death, he lowered himself, serving everyone around him.

By human standards, he started his priestly service as a complete failure. He held the same menial job for forty years. He never owned anything. As far as the world was concerned, he was unimportant. By spiritual standards, however, he was extremely successful. Tens of thousands benefited from his personal counsel and his miracles. Solanus Casey was one of the most prolific wonder-workers in Christian history. When he died in 1957, he was internationally famous. In one and a half days, twenty thousand people filed past his casket to say farewell to their beloved friend. One of his miracles had touched each of them in some way.

Solanus would have brushed off my high praise, if he even understood it. Every miracle amazed him. He saw each one as God's work, not his. He wept in awe with those who received miraculous healings. He never thought of himself as a miracle worker; he rarely thought of himself at all.

By age twenty-one, Barney Casey was an accomplished, practical man. As a teenager, he had been one of the mainstays of his large Midwestern family. He had already worked as a farmhand, lumberjack, brick maker, prison guard, motorman, and streetcar conductor. Then, in 1891, he witnessed a tragedy that set his life on a new course.

One cold, rainy afternoon as his streetcar rounded a curve in a rough part of town, it nearly hit a crowd of people gathered on the tracks. He brought it to a screeching halt, disembarked, and pushed through the crowd. But Barney was not prepared for the grisly scene he found there. A young, drunken sailor stood cursing over a young woman he had raped and stabbed repeatedly. The memory of this violent incident was seared in Barney's brain. He began to pray daily for the girl and the sailor, and then he felt that he must also pray for the whole world. He gradually came to see this event as a type of the evil afflicting all human beings. From that time, young Barney searched his soul for a way he could be of greater service in the world. Finally, he decided he could best use his life to help others by becoming a priest. That very year he entered the seminary of the diocese of Milwaukee.

As a seminarian, Barney was only a mediocre student. Perhaps he struggled academically because the texts were in Latin but most of the instructors taught in German, a language he had never mastered. For whatever reason, the seminary authorities told Casey in 1895 that he could not complete his studies there. They advised him to pursue his vocation as a lay brother in a religious order.

Frustrated but not defeated, Casey entered the Capuchin order in 1896. The Capuchins were a branch of the Friars Minor, which St. Francis founded in the thirteenth century. In 1897, Barney completed his novitiate at St. Bonaventure Monastery in Detroit, Michigan. As was their custom, the Capuchins gave him a new name, placing him under the patronage of St. Francis Solanus, a seventeenth-century missionary. From that time Barney was known as Solanus Casey. He spent the next seven years studying at the Capuchin seminary in Milwaukee. As at the diocesan seminary where he first began his studies, his books were in Latin and his classes in German.

In 1902, failure threatened Solanus again because some of the seminary professors were opposed to his ordination. But Father Anthony, the elderly seminary director, championed him. "We shall ordain Father Solanus," he said, "and as a priest, he will be to the people something like the Curé of Ars." St. John Vianney, the Curé of Ars, had been an extremely poor student but became a great confessor and wonder-worker. Little did the old priest realize how prophetic his words were.

When the time came for ordination in 1904, however, the seminary chose to limit Casey's priestly ministry. They decided he would be a "simplex priest"—he could not administer the sacrament of penance or preach formally. Nor could he wear the hood from which the Capuchins took their name. These restrictions would have shattered others, but Solanus seems to have accepted them peacefully.

During the fifty-three years of his priestly ministry, Father Solanus Casey never heard a confession, preached a mission, or conducted a retreat. He spent forty of those years as a porter, answering the door and greeting visitors to the monastery. That humble service provided the opportunity for his phenomenal career as a spiritual adviser and wonder-worker. Had he been given the full faculties of an ordinary priest, thousands might have been denied the graces of his friendship.

Father Solanus spent the first fifteen years of his priesthood quietly performing his duties at friaries in Yonkers and Manhattan. He was transferred in 1921 to Our Lady of the Angels Friary, Harlem, New York, then mainly a middle-class white community. It was at Our Lady of the Angels that he first became known as a counselor and miracle worker. Visitors to the monastery soon discovered that the new porter was a patient listener who gave sound and inspiring counsel. Many would come just to speak with Father Solanus.

One of his assignments was the promotion of the Seraphic Mass Association. Capuchins used this association worldwide as a means of intercessory prayer. It was named in honor of St. Francis of Assisi, who near the end of his life had a vision of a seraph, a six-winged member of heaven's highest order of angels. Capuchins everywhere prayed at their daily worship for those enrolled in the association. Shortly after Solanus started signing people up, extraordinary things began to happen. Reports of spiritual and physical healings streamed in. People were being healed of all sorts of ailments —pneumonia, heart disease, memory loss, insanity, lameness, cataracts, polio, alcoholism, gangrene, and blindness, to name just a few.

In November 1923, the Capuchin superior directed Solanus to keep a record of the miracles. Eight months later, the superior transferred Casey to St. Bonaventure's in Detroit, the Midwestern Capuchin headquarters, where he could keep a close eye on the wonder-worker. In short order the new porter and his gifts attracted an ever-increasing following. Solanus began to lead a Wednesday afternoon healing service, and many people faithfully came to benefit from his prayers. For the next two decades, people from all over the world trekked to St. Bonaventure's to receive the porter's ministry.

23

Solanus briefly noted thousands of miracles in his ledgers. We can consider only a few examples here.

William had long contemplated suicide. Solanus's notes do not give a reason for William's despondency, but after much suffering, he concocted a careful plan for taking his life. He would book passage on a boat traveling from Detroit to Cleveland and, as unobtrusively as possible, throw himself overboard along the way. His two sisters, who somehow got wind of his decision, kept him under close watch. Although riddled with fear for their brother, they didn't know what to do.

During this critical time, William's father died, magnifying his distress and therefore his danger. At the funeral, however, one of his sisters happened to find a pamphlet that mentioned the work of Solanus Casey. That very day she visited the priest and asked for his intercession on behalf of her troubled brother. Just four days later, the sister returned to tell Solanus that William had miraculously changed. Not only had he been suddenly released from his despair, she reported, but he was "praying, and full of hope," and making plans to go back to work.

Immediately the sisters sought the priest's prayer for another brother, who had tuberculosis. Six months later, Solanus recorded in his ledger of miracles that the man had entirely recovered from the disease.

Raymond was an eight-month-old infant afflicted in both ears with a serious infection called mastoiditis. Before the days of sophisticated antibiotics, this disease was life threatening. One evening, when the baby's fever skyrocketed, he was hospitalized. The doctor planned to perform a dangerous surgery the next morning to save his life. He would drill holes in the bone behind each ear for drainage, the pre-scribed treatment for mastoiditis at the time.

The infant's mother was crazed with fear, and when the hospital personnel were preoccupied, she smuggled Raymond from the building. Outside, she slipped into a waiting car, which her brother was driving, and they headed for home. Later, she told Solanus that she scarcely knew what she was doing at the time.

As they drove along the road, Raymond's mother suddenly recalled something about a priest at St. Bonaventure's who could heal people. *Why had she not thought of it before?* "Drive to the monastery," she told her brother.

When they arrived, she carried Raymond straight to Solanus, who sat alone in his office near the door. The priest stood and extended his arms to receive the infant while Raymond's mother told Solanus all that had happened—the disease, the planned surgery, the frantic escape. "O Father, help him," she sobbed.

Solanus handed Raymond back to his mother. He asked her to tell him the child's name and then entered it for intercessory prayer by the Seraphic Mass Association. Solanus then urged the mother to trust God and promised that he would not fail her. After that, he prayed over the infant.

"He will be better by morning," said Solanus, and at the door he assured her, almost casually, "And don't worry. He won't need an operation."

At home she placed Raymond in his crib near her own bed. She touched his little face and could feel the raging fever; then, exhausted, she fell asleep for several hours. When she awakened, she picked up the baby and pressed him to her breast. Raymond was cold and motionless. For a moment she feared that he had died. But then she felt him breathing and realized that he was in a deep sleep. Raymond seemed to be out of danger.

She and her husband whispered a prayer of thanks and then headed to tell Solanus the good news of Raymond's sudden recovery. The priest showed no surprise. When the couple tried to thank him, he told them to express their gratitude to God. The next day, the doctors examined Raymond and declared that no operation was necessary, inasmuch as he had returned to normal health.

25

By the hundreds, suffering people came to St. Bonaventure's to unload their burdens onto the stout spiritual shoulders of this saintly priest. Some sought life direction. Many wanted relief from problems—failures at work, disloyalty of friends or relatives, and the like. Others needed help pacifying family squabbles. Many came seeking healing for themselves or for loved ones. Solanus always responded with gentle, commonsensical advice and compassionate warmth that soothed petitioners. He would then enroll them in the Seraphic Mass Association, pray for them, exhort them to trust God, and send them off with a word of encouragement.

It is hardly surprising that Solanus Casey paid an enormous personal price in his service. He typically worked twelve-hour days, praying during the time he was not counseling guests. At night, he was often found in the chapel, sound asleep before the altar. Once, a brother observed that he chose a rather hard bed. "Don't worry about me," said Solanus. "I'm sleeping on the soft side of the planks."

He occasionally found the daily litany of people's suffering difficult to bear. "Sometimes," he wrote, "it becomes monotonous and extremely boring, till one is nearly collapsing; but in such cases, it helps to remember that even when Jesus was about to fall the third time he patiently consoled the womenfolk and children of his persecutors, making no exceptions. How can we ever be as grateful as we ought to be for such a vocation—for such privileged positions?"

And how can we be grateful enough for saints like Solanus Casey?

You may wonder why Solanus has no "St." before his name. That is because the Roman Catholic Church has yet to complete the process of formally recognizing him as a saint. But he is well on his way to receiving that recognition. Even if he were never acknowledged thus, however, I would always think of him as St. Solanus Casey.

Reflections of God

If the moon is beautiful as it reflects the light of the sun at so great a distance, what will be the beauty of the saints who for all eternity and not at a distance, will reflect the divine image of God!

Solanus Casey

PART TWO

MIRACULOUS PRAYER

I myself taught Ephraim to walk,
I myself took them by the arm,
but they did not know
    that I was the one caring for them,
that I was leading them with human ties,
with leading-strings of love,
that, with them, I was like someone
    lifting an infant to his cheek,
and that I bent down to feed him.

HOSEA 11:3–4, NJB

ontemporary believers diligently search for the supernatural. Many take endless journeys, seeking God everywhere. "People behave as though God has gotten lost," says Dominican theologian Augustine DiNoia, "and we must send out search parties to find him." Or we feel that God hides himself and even stands aloof from us. Somehow we believe that we must pursue him aggressively if we hope to touch him and let him touch us.

Do you think that's true? Are we the hunters and God the prize? Or is it just the opposite—God hounds us until we let him find us?

That's the way it was with the saints. Take St. Lutgarde, for example. Friends surrounded this effervescent, beautiful young woman. Many tempting distractions competed for her attention. She gave little thought to God until he caught up to her.

Consider St. Anthony of Egypt. He lived as a wealthy young landowner before God took hold of him and transformed him into one of history's most passionate and colorful saints.

God, the cosmic gem merchant, regarded Lutgarde and Anthony as pearls of great value, and he desired them above all. Isn't that the way it is with us? Don't we sometimes run, covering our tracks as we go, until God finds us? I love knowing that God values me enough to pursue me. It does wonders for my self-image. Now if only I can slow down long enough to let him overtake me.

Mystics have let God catch them and hold them close. That's why they can converse with him so intimately. St. Catherine of Siena could talk candidly to Jesus and expect him to do whatever she asked. Sometimes she even complained angrily to him. I can imagine the Lord smiling back affectionately at his tough little Italian favorite. When St. Clare of Assisi asked him for favors, he granted them. Her intercession healed her sick sisters and turned away would-be invaders of Assisi.

Most of us will never experience mystical phenomena. No raptures, ecstasies, or other preternatural events will overtake us. I don't know about you, but I'm grateful for that, because mystical consolations come at a great personal cost that I am not sure I'm ready to pay. However, we can permit God to lift us up, embrace us, press us to his cheek, feed us, teach us to walk in his way, lead us with human ties of love, and listen to our prayers. Wouldn't you consider that to be miraculous? I would.

Miracles That Made Peace

St. Catherine of Siena (1347–80)

By this all men will know that you are my disciples, if you love one another.

John 13:35

We celebrate Catherine of Siena as an international political figure, a feminist hero, and a doctor of the church. We think of her as Eleanor Roosevelt with a halo. We envision her dressed in a fourteenth-century tailored suit, traversing Europe to tell popes and emperors how to conduct their business.

This portrayal of Catherine contains a germ of truth. But only a germ. Catherine did work mightily to reconcile warring popes and emperors. She did most of that work, however, through letters and on her knees.

To get a more accurate view of Catherine, imagine a scruffy, not-so-respectable version of Mother Teresa. Catherine was not a nun, however, but a member of the Dominican Third Order. Thus she followed the life pattern of the Friars Preachers as a layperson. Think of her as an old-fashioned Italian matriarch, pious but sharp-tongued, who scandalized as many people as she influenced. Picture this short, frail lady, garbed in worn, rough clothes, in some of her typical daily activities, which included:

- Managing a large household of followers, all of whom called her "Mama."
- Living in poverty and begging with her disciples for everything they needed.
- Fasting severely but always seeing that her friends were well fed. Cooking food, baking bread, and sometimes praying for a miraculous multiplication or delivery of food.
- Praying for many hours at a time, at times seeming to become weightless when deep in prayer. People claim to have seen her floating a few inches off the ground.

31

- Reading the thoughts and knowing the temptations of her associates, even at long distances. She saw people's secret sins and confronted these people, urging them to repent. She touched hearts so effectively that the Friars Preachers had to designate three priests to handle the confessions of her penitents.
- Interceding fiercely for hardened criminals in Siena's jails. Even blasphemous prisoners embraced the gospel when she visited them.
- Caring for the sick. God healed plague victims when she prayed for them or touched them.
- Finally, offering advice to popes and princes. However, she was not so much an international politician as she was a spiritual director, and her venue was not the entire world but a small quadrant in northern Italy. The issue that concerned her most was not governmental but ecclesiastical. Catherine's passion was for the unity of the church.

32

In 1376, Catherine worked to repair a breach between Pope Gregory XI and a league of northern Italian cities led by Florence. Since 1305, the papacy had been a cause of contention between the French and the Italians. Turmoil in Rome and conflict with the emperor had forced the popes to retreat to Avignon in southern France. Catherine shared the popular Italian desire to restore the papacy to Rome. Pope Gregory XI was willing to make the move, but his powerful French advisers resisted.

Catherine conducted a campaign of letters to all sides and offered to mediate directly. She wrote Pope Gregory XI six times, exhorting him to return to Rome. The pope said that Catherine addressed him with an "intolerably dictatorial tone, a little sweetened with expressions of her perfect Christian deference." Encouraged by the Florentines, she went to Avignon on a peacemaking mission.

Apparently the pope had made a secret vow to move back to Rome, and this vow was revealed to Catherine. When she met the pope at Avignon, she didn't hesitate to use that inspired bit of information to pressure him. "Keep the promise you have made," she urged, to his great surprise. Not long after this encounter, Gregory XI returned the papacy to Rome. Catherine's efforts to reconcile the pope and the Italian cities finally succeeded during the reign of Urban VI, Gregory's successor.

More than anything, a dual passion for God and for the welfare of others consumed Catherine. As she pursued these passions, miracles happened.

Once, Catherine prayed for two condemned prisoners, who were then profoundly touched by God. Here's how it happened: Siena's magistrates had sentenced two hardened criminals to a brutal public death. They were driven about town in a cart while executioners tore at their bodies with red-hot pincers. The condemned men showed no trace of remorse for their crimes and roared curses and blasphemies at the people who lined the streets. They had refused to speak with the priests who had offered to prepare them for death.

Providentially for the prisoners, Catherine happened that day to be visiting a friend who lived on one of the roads the cart had to travel. "Mama, look at this horrible sight," said the woman as the tumultuous parade went by. While Catherine stood at the window observing the terrible scene, she was moved by compassion. In her mind's eye, she saw a mob of demons ready to punish the condemned men even more sadistically in hell.

Immediately she began to pray for the two unfortunates. "My most merciful Lord," she said with her characteristic frankness, "why do you show such contempt for your own creatures? Why are you letting them suffer such torture now? And even more vicious torture by these hellish spirits?" Catherine never beat around the bush, even in conversations with God.

To the amazement of all, both criminals suddenly stopped shouting curses and cried out for a priest. They wept and confessed their

33

sins to him. The crucified Christ, they claimed, had appeared to them urging repentance and offering forgiveness. They told the crowd that they expected to be with Christ in heaven, and then they submitted peacefully to their execution. This miraculous turn of events mystified the whole town, but Catherine's close friends knew that she had intervened in some way. For many days after the dramatic conversions, she was heard to say, "Thanks, Lord, for saving them from a second prison."

POWERFUL PRAYER
St. John Climacus (c. 579–c. 649)

Prayer is union with God and colloquy with him.

Prayer maintains the equilibrium of the world, reconciles people to God, produces holy tears, forms a bridge over temptations, and acts as a buttress between us and affliction.

Prayer drives away the struggles of the spirit. It is the blessedness to come. It is an action that will never come to an end.

Prayer is a spring of the virtues, it is an illumination of the mind, it is a curtain to shut out despair, it is a sign of hope, it is a victory over depression.

Prayer is a mirror in which we see our steps forward, it is a signpost of the route to follow, it is an unveiling of good things to come, it is a pledge of glory.

Prayer, for one who prays truly, is the soul's tribunal, it is the Lord's judgment on that person now, in advance of the final judgment.

Prayer is the queen of the virtues which summons us with a loud voice and says to us again: "Come to me all who labor and are heavy laden and I will give you perfect rest! Take my yoke upon you! You will find peace for your souls and healing for your wounds! For my yoke is easy and can restore the greatest fall" [see Matthew 11:28–30].

Let your prayer be very simple. For the tax collector and the prodigal son just one word was enough to reconcile them with God.

St. Raymond of Capua, Catherine's spiritual director and biographer, assisted her in another notable conversion. A celebrated rascal named Nanni di Ser Vanni specialized in stirring up private feuds. His plots often led to violent outbursts, and once one of his schemes resulted in a murder. No one could pin any charges on Nanni, but the whole town was wary of him. Raymond said that Nanni was so slippery that he would trick God if he could.

Catherine wanted a chance to persuade Nanni to change his ways, but he avoided her, said Raymond, as "the snake avoids the charmer." One of her disciples, however, convinced Nanni to visit her and to listen to what she had to say. Nanni thought he would hear her out and then go about his business. He had no idea what he was in for.

Raymond was present when Nanni met Catherine. She greeted him politely, offered him a seat, and asked why he had come.

"I came," he said, "because I promised a mutual friend that I would. He asked me to tell you the truth about my affairs, and I will. But don't imagine that you can make me stop."

Then Nanni candidly admitted that he was behind several murderous plots presently seething in Siena. In her typical blend of sweetness and sharpness, Catherine warned him that his soul was in mortal danger, but Nanni adamantly refused to change his behavior.

When Catherine realized that he had turned a deaf ear, she began to pray quietly and then immediately drifted into an ecstasy. Raymond covered for her and picked up the conversation. Shortly, Nanni found himself talking about his machinations. He described one feud in detail and expressed his willingness to let Raymond quell that disturbance.

Then an extraordinary thing happened. Nanni made a move to leave, but remorse overwhelmed him. "My God," he said, "how contented I feel in my soul from having said I shall make peace! Lord God, what is this power that draws me? I can't go and I can't say no." After that, he promised to do anything Catherine directed him to do to set things right.

Catherine awakened and said, "I spoke to you, and you would not listen, so I spoke to God and *he* got your attention." Then she gently urged Nanni to make peace with God, which he did on the spot.

Over the next few weeks, she helped him reconcile with all his enemies, and from that time on Nanni lived an upright life. The scoundrel had experienced a complete personal transformation. Later on, to express his gratitude, he deeded to Catherine a castle near Siena, which she turned into a convent.

When the plague struck Siena, Catherine and her friends courageously tended the sick. The disease eventually struck Matteo, the rector of the city's hospital and a close friend of Catherine. When she got the news, she hurried off to see him. She was hot with anger at the plague, and even before she reached his bed she began shouting from a distance: "Get up, Matteo, get up! This is not time for lying in a soft bed!" At this command, Matteo's fever, swelling, and pain disappeared.

Catherine slipped away to avoid attracting attention. Just then Raymond—unaware of the miracle—approached and begged her to pray for Matteo's recovery.

"What?" exclaimed Catherine, pretending to be offended. "Do you think I am God that I can deliver someone from death?"

"Don't give me that!" said Raymond. "I know that Jesus does whatever you ask him to."

Catherine smiled mischievously. "Cheer up," she said. "He won't die this time."

A short time later, Raymond shared a hearty celebration meal with Matteo, who a few hours before could barely open his mouth.

One day in Catherine's neighborhood, a balcony collapsed, hurtling a woman to the ground. The victim lived near Catherine, and they were friends. Falling debris had so badly cut and bruised the woman that she could not move. Catherine visited her injured friend and tried to comfort her. In a soothing gesture, she touched the woman, and the pain immediately left that spot. The woman begged Catherine to touch another place that hurt. There, too, the pain vanished. So they kept it up—the woman requesting that Catherine touch injured places until all the pain was gone. The woman had recovered completely. "Catherine," she told everyone, "has cured me by touching me."

Once, on a visit to Pisa, Catherine found herself in a seriously weakened condition. Raymond of Capua and other friends sought a remedy to strengthen her. They searched for some vernaccia, a wine with healing properties. Vernaccia was supposed to bring relief when applied to a sick person's temples and wrists. Catherine's friends asked a neighbor who always stocked vernaccia to give them a decanter. "I would gladly give you the barrel if I had it," he said, "but it has been empty for three months." For emphasis, he pulled the spigot from the barrel and then stared in amazement as wine gushed forth. So Catherine's friends miraculously obtained medicine for her.

To Catherine's great embarrassment, news of the miracle spread throughout Pisa. She was back on her feet in a few days, and people greeted her excitedly. "Well, what do you know," someone teased. "You don't drink wine but you can fill an empty cask with it!"

The hubbub displeased Catherine. "O Lord," she prayed with near-irreverent familiarity, "why have you willed to inflict me with the pain of this mockery? Who asked you for the wine, anyway? For a long time I've deprived my body of wine, but now wine is making a joke of me. By your infinite mercy, have pity on me! Do something and put an end to this chatter."

The wine turned as sour as vinegar and was no longer potable. The owner of the miracle barrel and those who came to sample the wine stopped talking about it. Catherine was delighted.

In 1378, Christendom was torn by the Great Western Schism. Two men claimed to be the pope, one based at Avignon and the other at Rome. Catherine spent herself in prayer and advocacy on behalf of

Urban VI, who called her to advise him in Rome. Her intensive efforts to win support for him wore heavily on her. In 1380, Catherine had a vision in which the church, depicted as a great ship, seemed to crush her. Her response to this vision was to pray and offer her suffering on behalf of the church. A few months later, in April, she died of a paralytic stroke.

I liked Catherine of Siena when I knew her superficially as an ambassador who straightened out affairs of church and state. I admire her more now that I have become better acquainted with her. She was a sweet curmudgeon, like several of my Italian aunts. The beatitude says, "Blessed are the peacemakers, for they shall be called children of God." That text sums up Catherine's life perfectly.

Unselfish Love

God said: I have placed you in the midst of your fellows that you may do to them what you cannot do to me, that is to say that you may love your neighbor freely without expecting any return from him, and what you do to him I count as done to me.

Dialogue of St. Catherine of Siena

The "Accidental" Mystic

St. Lutgarde of Aywières (1182–1246)

The charm of St. Lutgarde is heightened by a certain earthly simplicity. Lutgarde for all her ardent and ethereal mysticism, remained always a living human being of flesh and bone.

Thomas Merton

Lutgarde became a saint by "accident." Her father squandered her dowry in a bad business deal, and her wealthy mother financed her entry into a convent. In 1194, at age twelve, Lutgarde went to live at the Benedictine monastery of St. Catherine, situated near Saint-Trond, located in present-day Belgium, close to Liège and the Meuse River.

At first, Lutgarde simply boarded at St. Catherine's, coming and going as she pleased. She even entertained young men as guests. She viewed these as innocent friendships, and she seemed flattered by the attention. One young fellow, however, fell in love with her. He even tried to persuade her to run off with him.

One day as this admirer whispered sweet nothings to Lutgarde, Christ himself intervened. He appeared to her in a blazing vision and showed her the wound in his side. "Stop seeking the pleasure of this unbecoming affection," he said. "See here, forever, what you should love, and how you should love."

Stunned and terrified, Lutgarde abruptly dismissed her astonished suitor. "Get away from me, you bait of death," she said. "I belong to another Lover." In that moment she set the course of her life. She began to pray more seriously and do penance more rigorously. The nuns at St. Catherine's observed Lutgarde's conversion icily, doubting that this worldly girl would have much stick-to-itiveness.

The sisters soon had to admit their mistake. Not only did Lutgarde persevere in prayer, but she also learned to speak with Christ quite familiarly. When the nuns interrupted her with tasks, she would say, "Wait here, Lord Jesus. I'll come right back as soon as I'm finished." The sisters' skepticism melted when they observed Lutgarde's

39

personal worship. At such times, they felt their hearts mysteriously warmed by the radiance that seemed to flow from her.

Lutgarde's divine favors did not impress her. She had received, for example, a gift of healing. When word about it spread, hosts of petitioners came to her for healing of minor illnesses. Lutgarde became increasingly annoyed with these requests because they interrupted her prayer. "Why did you go and give me such a grace, Lord?" she asked. "Take it away, please!" Then she impishly added, "But give me something better!"

As an alternative, Lutgarde requested a miraculous understanding of Latin. Throughout the day the sisters used that language in choir for chanting psalms and prayers. Lutgarde prayed fervently but did not grasp a word of what she was saying, so she thought that a greater understanding of the texts would magnify her devotion. The Lord granted the grace and enabled Lutgarde to understand the Latin words. But to her disappointment, this enlightenment did not enhance her worship, as the light did not seem to get from her head to her heart.

40

Lutgarde again complained to the Lord. Her new intellectual gift, she said, depleted her prayer instead of strengthening it. "What, then, do you want?" the Lord seemed to ask.

"Lord," she said, "I want your heart." She thought she heard Jesus reply, "But Lutgarde, I want *your* heart."

"Take my heart," Lutgarde prayed in response. "May your heart's love be so mingled and united with my heart that I may possess my heart in you. May it ever remain there safe in your protection." In Lutgarde's first vision, Christ had shown her his heart. Now it seemed to her that he linked his heart so closely with hers that she shared his core desires. From then on Lutgarde felt that she participated in Christ's deepest longing—his desire to redeem sinful human beings. This passionate, Christ-inspired charity shaped the rest of her life.

Lutgarde's ascent to mystical heights did not go to her head. She never became arrogant or otherworldly. Her simplicity, friendliness, and generosity authenticated her spirituality and won the trust and affection of her sisters. In 1205, these nuns, who had once thought Lutgarde would never make it, named her prioress of St. Catherine's.

This election horrified Lutgarde because her new duties took her away from prayer. It prompted her to seek a place in another monastery. In 1206, she moved to a Cistercian house in Aywières that was secluded in a lovely valley near Brussels. Aywières appealed to Lutgarde because it was both austere and exclusively French speaking. There she could practice her spiritual disciplines with no danger of being drafted for community office. Happy that she spoke only Flemish, Lutgarde was not about to pray for the grace to understand French!

For the next forty years, Lutgarde prayed and did penance to support Christ's purposes. She saw herself as a partner with Christ in his work. Three times at Aywières Lutgarde undertook seven-year fasts in reparation for others' sins. The first time, she subsisted on bread and liquids as she prayed for the Cathars, heretics who held that the material world was evil and who denied that Jesus was a human being. Lutgarde believed that Christ commissioned her second seven-year fast as an offering on behalf of sinners at large.

Near the end of her life, Lutgarde went on a third seven-year fast, during which she prayed for protection of the church from Emperor Frederick II's efforts to destroy it. She prophesied that "either the prayers of the faithful would humble this man who secretly desires the overthrow of the church, or else he will soon depart this life and leave the church in peace." Both prophecies were fulfilled a few years after her death: Frederick II was first deposed, and then he died suddenly in 1250.

St. Lutgarde's graceful tenderness endeared her to the sisters at Aywières. She always had kind words for the troubled and sensible advice for the perplexed. The nuns loved her for it. She never forgot others' needs, even when she was at prayer.

Once, after receiving communion, Lutgarde was enjoying a pleasant reverie in Christ's presence. Her very sick friend Sister Elizabeth languished nearby in the infirmary. Elizabeth's affliction had so weakened her that she was confined to bed, and the other sisters had to feed her at frequent intervals, day and night. As Lutgarde prayed, suppertime approached, and she became hungry. The spunky nun then prayed, "Lord, I am enjoying this time with you, but I am getting hungry. Why don't you go to Elizabeth and take possession of her heart? Let me go get something to eat and build up my strength." So Lutgarde went off to eat, and Elizabeth was suddenly strengthened. She not only did not *need* any food, but she could not even eat for some time. Soon she was completely well and returned to full community life.

On another occasion, Lutgarde came late to choir. She found Sister Matilda, who was deaf, weeping because she could not hear the beautiful singing. Overcome with compassion for her friend, Lutgarde knelt and prayed briefly. Then she wet her fingers with spittle and put them in Matilda's ears. Matilda felt something snap, and her ears were suddenly filled with the voices of sopranos chanting the psalms. Paradoxically, Lutgarde did not seek healing for herself. Eleven years before her death in 1246, she lost her sight. She cherished the blindness as a blessing that removed her from distracting worldly involvements.

I first heard of St. Lutgarde of Aywières when I discovered Thomas Merton's biography of the saint in a friend's library. I'm glad I met this lovely woman. Her tenacious idealism, rigorous asceticism, and fervent mysticism intimidate me, I confess. But I revere her for them. And Lutgarde's affectionate attention to others has charmed me along with Thomas Merton and the sisters at Aywières.

A Tiger Lily of a Saint

In the month of June, when the sun burns high in the bright firmament and when Cistercian monks, like all other farmers, hitch up their teams and go out to gather in the wheat, St. Lutgarde's Day comes around. She is a saint whose spirit is as ardent and colorful as the June weather and as bright as the tiger lilies that enliven the fields and roadsides in the month in which we celebrate her memory.

Thomas Merton

Miracles in the Desert

ST. ANTHONY OF EGYPT (C. 251–356)

Anthony was like a good physician given to the people of Egypt. For whoever came to him afflicted who did not go away rejoicing? Whoever came to him full of rage who was not enriched with graciousness and long-suffering? And what person ever came to him troubled in mind who did not go away with it composed? . . . People loved him so much that after he had departed from this world, his memory never died. Everyone took courage from the repetition of his triumphs and of his words.

ST. ATHANASIUS

St. Anthony was not the first ascetic, but he was the first monk to flee the city to pursue God in the desert. Or perhaps to let God find and catch him there.

Ascetic comes from a Greek word for "athlete." Christian ascetics were spiritual athletes, and the Gospels were their workout programs. Prayer, fasting, and charitable works were their exercises. Jesus and Paul were their trainers. The Holy Spirit, as they often said, was their strength, while God was their prize, and they were his.

Anthony was born near Memphis in Egypt around 251. By then, many Christians had disengaged from ordinary life to devote themselves exclusively to God. Men and women alike had become hermits. The men were called "monks," taking their name from a Greek word for "solitary," and the women were "nuns," *nonnae* in Latin, meaning they said no to worldly desires. Some ascetics sought their solitude right in the middle of towns. For safety's sake, nuns stayed with their families or resided together in households, but many monks lived alone on the outskirts of cities in huts, caves, or abandoned tombs.

These ascetics pursued virtue by avoiding secular society while maintaining contact with their local Christian communities. They felt they had a lot to flee. The Roman Empire was lustful, violent, and brutish, and its culture made evil attractive. Monks and nuns abandoned these persuasively wicked environments because they believed that living apart helped them conquer their own evil tendencies.

Anthony was twenty when his parents died and left him responsible for his little sister. A few months later, at Mass one Sunday, the gospel changed his life. "If you want to be perfect," proclaimed the lector, "go, sell your possessions and give to the poor, and you will have treasure in heaven. Then come, follow me" (Matthew 19:21). Anthony was certain that God had spoken right to him. He responded by selling his parents' estate and the possessions he had inherited. He distributed the proceeds to the poor, reserving only enough to provide for his sister's future.

A short time later, Anthony heard the lector at another Sunday liturgy declare, "Do not worry about tomorrow" (Matthew 6:34). Again, he took the words personally and gave as alms the money he had set aside for his sister. He found the little girl a home with a household of nuns, the first convent in recorded history. Then he moved to a hut on the edge of town and became a hermit. Later on, he would pursue a solitary life in the Egyptian desert.

The young monk learned the ascetical life from other recluses who lived nearby on the outskirts of the city. Imitating their Christian behavior, he diligently applied their teachings on prayer and other spiritual practices. When he noticed a virtue in one of them, he worked at acquiring it. He pursued it doggedly until he had mastered the quality even more perfectly than his model had. St. Athanasius, Anthony's biographer, said that he "was a perfect handicraftsman in matters that related to fear of God."

Anthony developed a pattern that he followed for eighty-five years. He ate once a day, never before sunset, and his meal consisted of six ounces of bread soaked in water, sometimes seasoned with a little salt. When he was elderly, he occasionally allowed himself a few palm dates and a little oil. He wore sheepskin garments with the hair against his body. Weaving mats of palm fronds was his ordinary work. Later, when he moved to the desert, he tilled a small garden, growing wheat to make his bread and vegetables for his guests.

All day and all night, Anthony prayed. At any time, a visitor might find him rapt in mystical ecstasies. He loved to pray at night and sometimes complained that the sunrise robbed him of the greater light of inner contemplation.

Once, however, he became depressed because he did not feel strong enough for lengthy prayer. He took comfort from a vision in which an angel showed him the value of balancing prayer and work. The angel alternatively wove mats and then rose to pray. After a while, the angel said, "Do this, and you will find relief." So Anthony adjusted his pattern. However, St. Athanasius says, he continued to pray a little while he worked.

Anthony's monastic career progressed through three stages. For fifteen years he lived in huts and tombs near the village of Koman. Then, at age thirty-five, he withdrew to an isolated mountain in the Egyptian desert to escape the steady stream of people who sought him for miraculous cures. After twenty years, however, he entered a more active phase and left his mountain retreat to form communities of hermits in the desert. Occasionally he traveled into Alexandria to lend his personal support to the local Christians, who faced both persecution and heresy.

St. Athanasius reported that the devil opposed Anthony at every turn throughout his life. As a result, he became adept at spiritual warfare. As a young monk, he valiantly resisted temptations to lust and second thoughts about his vocation. The enemy also attacked Anthony by appearing in visible forms, once as a woman and then again as a strong young man. But he typically overcame the devil's phantasms by proclaiming the name of Jesus.

Athanasius said that once when Anthony had gone into the desert, the devil sent an army of wild animals to attack him. As they were about to pounce, the saint confronted them. "If the Lord has given you power over me," he shouted, "come and get it over with. But if Satan sent you, get out of here quickly, for I am a servant of Jesus." At the name "Jesus," the animals scattered. And, said Athanasius, Satan fled "like a sparrow before a hawk."

All of Egypt knew about Anthony's power over the devil, so many people flocked to him, seeking deliverance from evil spirits. Anthony, however, diverted attention from his gifts by requiring petitioners to exercise their own faith. Once, Martinianus, a Roman official, asked Anthony to release his daughter from possession by a demon. "Why do you bother me?" said Anthony. "I'm a man, just like you. But if you believe in Christ, whom I serve, go away and you'll receive your request." As Martinianus and his child made their way home, God touched the girl and set her free.

On another occasion, Parnîtôn, also an official, came with the claim that a demon was causing him to gnaw his tongue and to lose his sight. He wanted to stay with Anthony until he was healed, but the saint ordered him to leave. "You can't be healed here," he said. "Go back to Egypt. There you will see the wonderful sign God has worked for you." Parnîtôn obeyed, and before he reached home he was cured.

Anthony claimed no supernatural gift of healing, only inspired knowledge of God's interventions in people's lives. Once, a nun from the region of Busiris whose face was so afflicted with cancer that she had gone blind longed for Anthony to pray for her. Some relatives took her and joined company with a group of monks who were crossing the desert to visit him. When the entourage drew near the mountain where Anthony lived, the family and the nun stayed behind while the monks went on to see him.

Awestruck in Anthony's presence, the monks were hesitant to ask him to do something for the young woman. But he read their thoughts. Before they could say a word about her, he startled them by saying, "Go back to the place where you left the maiden, and you will find that she has been healed completely. This didn't happen through me or through any gift of mine. It's a gift from God, who heard the young lady's prayer and saw the faithful concern of her family. He revealed to me just now that he has cured her." Quickly, the monks returned to find the family celebrating gaily and the young nun's body restored, clean of any trace of cancer.

47

When he turned fifty-five, St. Anthony left the seclusion of his mountain retreat to found an informal community of solitaries who built huts near each other. A community of solitaries sounds like an oxymoron, doesn't it? It's a contradiction, however, only if we imagine that in his flight to the desert, Anthony rejected all relationships. Though he valued his solitude, he welcomed those who sought him out. Many ordinary people looking for miracles tracked him down in the most remote places. Monks came in large numbers to learn from him. Their appeals for help seem to have persuaded him to build a community in the wilderness.

Anthony's monks dwelled apart but gathered for prayer and teaching. Living alone together enabled them to help each other in their quest for holiness. According to Athanasius, Anthony taught his community about faith, love of God, discipline of the flesh, prayer, Scripture study, and reflection. His teaching, however, centered on loving one another, forgiveness, avoiding and repairing wrongdoing, and mutual accountability. Anthony wanted his brothers both to prize their relationship with God and to support it by learning to love one another.

Anthony also had a brotherly commitment to the Christians of Alexandria, with whom he maintained regular contact. He was the loyal friend of St. Athanasius, the bishop who wrote his life story. In 311, when the Roman Empire renewed its persecution of Christians, Anthony went to Alexandria to encourage the martyrs. Fearlessly, he put himself at great risk by appearing in the presence of the governor. Friends finally persuaded him to leave so as not to provoke an attack on himself.

Later, he used his immense popularity to oppose the Arian heresy. In the 330s, the Arians, who denied Jesus' divinity, were making inroads in Alexandria. At Athanasius's urging, Anthony went to the city in 339 to speak against the heresy. Crowds rallied around him, and he encouraged them to shun the heretics so that they might not be led astray by errors.

After this foray into the city, Anthony returned to the desert. He longed for the solitude and opportunities for contemplation. However, so many people sought his help that he was hardly ever alone. At the request of some monks, he founded another monastery. Officials came to consult him, philosophers to debate him, and petitioners to be healed. Anthony spent his last years loving God by loving others.

Remarkably, Anthony's lifelong austerity does not seem to have damaged his body. Even in his old age he appeared strong. "His eyes did not wax dim," said St. Athanasius, "and not one of his teeth dropped out, and both his feet and his hands were sound and healthy. Even though he ate so little, his appearance was more glorious than that of those who fed themselves on dainty meats."

Not bad for an old monk who reportedly had fasted every day for eighty-five years.

Acquiring Virtue

Let us continue to be strenuous in the pursuit of virtue. Let us not grow tired of seeking it, for our Lord has become a guide for us and for every person who has a desire for the virtues. And so that it might not be tedious for us, Saint Paul became our example when he said, "I die daily" [see 1 Corinthians 15:31]. Now, if we were to think each day that we had to die that day, we would never sin at all. This is the explanation of Paul's saying. . . . If we were to keep the imminence of our death in mind, we would never be overcome by sin: lust which is fleeting would not reign over us; we would never harbor anger against another human being; we would not love the possessions which pass away; and we would forgive every person who offended us. . . . Therefore, O my beloved, let us be zealous in carrying out the work we have committed ourselves to, and let us travel to the end on the road on which we have begun our journey.

St. Athanasius

49

Miracles to the Rescue
ST. CLARE OF ASSISI (C. 1193–1253)

What are the servants of God but his singers whose duty it is to lift up the hearts of men and women and move them to spiritual joy?

ST. FRANCIS OF ASSISI

A popular notion imagines that St. Clare and St. Francis of Assisi were romantically linked. *Brother Sun and Sister Moon,* a silly movie, helped spread this nonsense. It may make good fiction, but let's set the record straight.

Clare and Francis were not lovers.

They were not infatuated with each other.

They did not "hang out" together.

And they never slipped away for a lovers' rendezvous.

If you are looking for a medieval religious couple who were a "thing," stick with Héloïse and Abelard.

Eighteen-year-old Clare encountered Francis for the first time when she heard him preach at St. George's in Assisi. At the time, Clare was already a devoted Christian, but Francis's plain talk about Christ's love intensified her desire to live more fully for God. She decided she would find a way to imitate Francis's gospel pattern of life.

Clare met with Francis numerous times, always in the company of a close female friend. They visited clandestinely so as not to alarm her family. As notables in Assisi, Clare's parents expected her to marry well. She knew that when her family learned about her spiritual intentions, they would raise a furious storm of resistance. One relative, Rufino, had already shamed the family by joining Francis's band of beggars. Clare knew that her relatives would view her decision as an even more dishonorable defection. She would be throwing away her chance to advance the family's fortunes. Worse, she would be disgracing them by joining a disreputable movement that associated with Assisi's underclass.

Francis and Clare evidently agreed that she would start a women's community modeled on his friars. Very likely they consulted Bishop Guido of Assisi about Clare's vocation. He was Francis's early, enthusiastic protector, and the saint always sought his direction.

Clare and Francis set Palm Sunday, 1212, as the date that she would flee her family. That morning, Clare attended the liturgy as usual. Thomas of Celano, her biographer, described her as "resplendent with joy." He hinted that Clare regarded that Mass as her marriage to Christ. When everyone went forward to receive palm fronds, she stayed back with a bride's shyness. Bishop Guido noticed and carried a branch to her. Perhaps he winked his complicity as he offered her this little sign of encouragement.

In the evening, accompanied by a relative, Clare slipped away from her parents' home. Francis and his brothers welcomed her at the church of St. Mary of the Angels. Bearing torches and singing the "Veni Creator Spiritus," they proceeded into the chapel. There, Clare made her profession. "I want only Jesus Christ," she said, "and to live by the Gospel, owning nothing and in chastity." Francis sealed her vow by shearing her long, golden hair, and Clare traded her clothing for a coarse sackcloth habit.

Then the trouble began, as Clare's departure had precipitated a great scandal in Assisi. Decent but worldly people were enraged, judging her as selfish and headstrong. For Clare's security, Francis hid her nearby in a Benedictine convent. When her powerful uncle Monaldo discovered her whereabouts, he and a posse of her male relatives tried to forcibly remove her and bring her home. The angry men burst into the convent, where they found Clare in the chapel, clinging to the altar. She felt she would be safe there because they would be reluctant to invade the sanctuary and thus defile it. Finally, to show that nothing could make her change her mind, Clare startled the men by uncovering her shorn head. At that, her would-be kidnappers admitted the hopelessness of their effort and left.

A few days later, Agnes, Clare's fifteen-year-old sister, joined her at the convent. Shamed even more by the flight of one so young, an enraged Monaldo and his men again stormed the convent, demanding to see Agnes. When the frightened girl appeared, Monaldo shouted, "What do you think you are doing? You will come home with me right now!"

"I have decided to follow Christ and his Gospel with Clare," said Agnes. "I will never leave her."

At that, the men grabbed her and dragged her from the convent. Agnes screamed for help, neighbors came running, and Clare knelt in prayer. Then a marvelous thing happened in the sight of all. When one of the men stooped to lift Agnes and carry her off, he could not budge her. By divine intervention the girl had become so heavy that no one could move her. Exasperated, the men finally gave up. Clare's prayer had conquered them, and they left, never to return.

Francis gave Clare a little house contiguous with the vacant church of Saint Damian on the outskirts of Assisi. This became the base from which she built her community. Women from prominent local families soon joined her, Clare's mother among them. Within a few years, convents of Clare's sisters opened in Italy and France. Even Agnes of Bohemia renounced her proposed marriage to Emperor Frederick II to found a convent in that country.

Clare and her sisters joyfully lived a penitential life. They wore rough clothing, went barefoot, slept on the ground, fasted frequently, never ate meat, and never spoke unless it was necessary. Clare was devoted to "Lady Poverty." She wanted her community to own nothing and to live on daily contributions.

Although we do not remember Clare of Assisi as a miracle worker, God intervened in events on her behalf. Once, the convent was out of oil, a minor disaster in any Italian household. Clare washed a jar and placed it at the door. When the friar who begged on behalf of the sisters came for it, he was surprised to find it full of oil. On another occasion, Clare fed fifty sisters and all the friars with a single loaf of bread.

Clare also possessed a gift of healing. Thomas of Celano said that when Clare made the sign of the cross over people, she could cure their diseases. Once, St. Francis sent Stephen, a friar who was mentally ill, to Clare. She touched him, and he immediately recovered his senses. Three-year-old Mattiolo was brought to Clare with a pebble lodged in his nostril. She blessed him with the sign of the cross, and the stone fell out.

Clare also healed her sisters—Benevenuta, who had suffered for twelve years with open sores; Amata, of edema; Christiana, of deafness. One night another Benevenuta, who had been without her voice for two years, had a vision that Clare would heal her on the next day, and Clare did. On another occasion Clare walked into the infirmary, made the sign of the cross five times, and five sisters were immediately cured of their illnesses.

Twice Clare's courage and intercession miraculously saved Assisi. In 1241, Emperor Frederick II invaded northern Italy. Among the imperial troops were Saracens who ravaged the Spoleto valley where Assisi lay. Saint Damian was an easy target, sitting exposed on the edge of the town. Clare, although very sick, took bold action to defend her sisters. She confronted the raiders at the door with a silver box containing a consecrated host.

Prostrating herself, she prayed: "Does it please you, Lord, to deliver your defenseless handmaids into the hands of these pagans? I beg you, Lord, defend them for me, since I can't defend them myself." She also prayed for the protection of Assisi. Then a voice was heard to say, "I will always defend you," and at that the marauders clambered over the convent walls and fled.

Shortly after that, a general in the imperial army besieged Assisi. When it appeared that the city would fall, Clare and her sisters once again interceded for it. They removed their veils, covered their heads with ashes, and pleaded for the city's safety. Their prayer was answered swiftly. Overnight the army disbanded, and not long after, the general was killed.

For the last two decades of her life, Clare, the saint who cured others, was very sick. But she endured her infirmities with remarkable fortitude. On her deathbed, when a brother exhorted her to endure her final suffering patiently, she declared: "Ever since I have known the grace of my Lord Jesus Christ through his servant Francis, no suffering has troubled me, no penance has been hard, no sickness too arduous." She died in 1253.

Clare believed that her life and the lives of her sisters were "patterns and mirrors for those who live in the world." Do you see in her, as I do, a luminous reflection of Christ?

The Spotless Mirror

Happy the soul to whom it is given to attain this life with Christ, to cleave with all one's heart to Him:

> Whose beauty all the heavenly hosts behold forever,
> Whose love inflames our love,
> Whose contemplation is our refreshment,
> Whose graciousness is our delight,
> Whose gentleness fills us to overflowing,
> Whose remembrance gives sweet light,
> Whose fragrance revives the dead,
> Whose glorious vision will be the happiness of all the citizens of that heavenly Jerusalem.

For he is the brightness of eternal glory [see Hebrews 1:3], the splendor of eternal light, the mirror without spot [Wisdom 7:26].

St. Clare of Assisi

PART THREE

DREAMS, VISIONS, *and* OTHER WONDERS

But Stephen, full of the Holy Spirit, looked up to heaven and saw the glory of God, and Jesus standing at the right hand of God. "Look," he said, "I see heaven open and the Son of Man standing at the right hand of God."

ACTS 7:55–56

rank Sheed, the great Catholic apologist, defined *sanity* as being in touch with reality. On that ground he diagnosed most people as technically insane. He argued that because we confine our vision to the material world, we remain blind to the vast spiritual realm in which we live. Without seeing the world of the Spirit, strictly speaking, we become insane. That accounts for a lot of the craziness we observe in contemporary society.

Thank God for mystics, who see reality more completely than the rest of us do. Their closeness to the Lord allows them to move beyond the veil that shrouds us in the darkness of mere earthly things. Their experience testifies to the marvelous, but invisible, spiritual world that surrounds us. Their example and testimony offer a cure for our blindness and insanity.

St. Perpetua, a twenty-something Roman socialite, had her whole life ahead of her. However, this remarkable young woman, a recent convert to Christianity, looked beyond her comforts and desires to uphold the truth of her new faith. Onlookers at the arena must have thought her mad to choose death in the jaws of wild beasts. But the Lord had encouraged her with a vision of her victorious entry into heaven. So emboldened by an accurate perception of reality, Perpetua courageously faced her martyrdom.

Like most of us, St. Gertrude the Great suffered from emotional stress and doubts that tried her soul. But the Lord opened the eyes of her heart with visions of his tender love for her. With an enviable spiritual sanity, she allowed Christ to sweep her off her feet and to place her firmly in his presence, where she seems to have remained continuously.

No other modern mystic testifies to the reality of the spiritual world more than Blessed Padre Pio. Like Jesus himself, he possessed the mysterious ability to break through the limits of the material world and open people to spiritual reality. He read consciences, foretold events, appeared in two places at once, healed the sick, raised the dead, and for half a century bore Christ's wounds on his body. I think that God sent him to the world as a spiritual wake-up call.

Mystics remind me of the centurion who asked Jesus to heal his servant (see Matthew 8:5–13). This Italian warrior was more in touch with spiritual reality than the Twelve ever were. He astonished the Lord by saying, "You don't need to come to my house. Just say the word and my servant shall be healed." Somehow this unlikely disciple realized that the Word of God, not "laws of nature," governed the universe. Mystics also apprehend this truth, and their faith and obedience also astonish Jesus. Just as he did for the centurion, he says yes to their prayers. Miracles result and open our eyes to the real world. We may even imitate the faith and obedience of mystics like Perpetua, Gertrude, and Padre Pio. Then we too may astonish the Lord.

Visions

St. Perpetua (c. 181–203)

You must all stand fast in the faith and love one another. And do not be weakened by what we have gone through.

St. Perpetua

Just before Perpetua was martyred, she wrote a touching account of her last days. History has kindly preserved this remarkable personal document for us, and when I read her words, I become enchanted with this wonderful woman. Perpetua seems to pour out her heart to me, and I feel as though I am visiting her in prison. But instead of me comforting her, she is encouraging me. I would have counted myself fortunate to be one of her friends.

Maybe I feel close to Perpetua because I know several women who resemble her—an intriguing blend of seriousness and fun. No doubt you know women like her: vivacious and lovely, their eyes bright with affection—women who stir admiration in everyone.

Women like Perpetua radiate inner strength. I call them "velvet bricks" because their character mixes gentleness with pluck. On the outside, tender, accessible, and soft. On the inside, single-hearted, determined, and strong. Such women competently control the things around them. Awestruck, people stand back and let them take the lead.

59

Perpetua lived in Carthage, North Africa, at the end of the second century. She was a wealthy woman, the wife of a prominent man, and the mother of an infant son. Her mother and brother were probably Christians. Her father, a dyed-in-the-wool pagan, loved her as his favorite child.

At age twenty-two, Perpetua decided to become a Christian. She and four friends received instructions in the faith from Saturus, their catechist. Her companions were Secundulus, Saturninus, and the slaves Revocatus and Felicity, who was in the last month of her pregnancy. In 203, just as they were preparing for baptism, Emperor Severus launched a general persecution. Anyone who refused to worship him as a god was threatened with capital punishment.

Apparently because of their recent conversion to Christianity, Perpetua and the others were suspect. The local governor had them all arrested and confined to a private house while awaiting examination. Saturus, who was not with his five pupils when they were taken, would not let them face their trial alone. He marked himself for death by voluntarily joining them in their confinement.

The new Christians were all young, brimful with idealism, and strong of character, but they were not vaccinated against fear. Imagine the terrible thoughts that must have preyed upon Felicity. What would become of her unborn child? Would the child survive her? Or would her little innocent die a violent death with her? Perhaps she even considered not sticking to her choice to become a Christian. After all, what was a little incense offered to a conceited emperor if it spared her child? Whatever tempting thoughts might have plagued Felicity's mind, however, she did not buckle.

Terrors must also have afflicted doughty Perpetua, no matter how brave she was. The arrest had separated her from her infant son, whom she was still nursing. Her swollen breasts must have constantly reminded her of the pain she was causing her son. Certainly, her heart ached to hold and cuddle him again. Like Felicity, she must have entertained horrible fears about her baby's future. Would he be well cared for? Would he someday hate her memory because she had abandoned him?

The idea of Perpetua's death seemed to drive her father mad, and he made things a lot harder for her. Perpetua loved her father deeply and sorrowed over his torment. One day he visited her and begged her to change her mind about becoming a Christian.

"Father," she said, pointing to a water jug, "do you see this container? Can it be called by any other name than what it is—a jug?"

"No," he replied.

"And just so, I cannot call myself by any other name than what I am—a Christian."

At the word *Christian,* he quivered with rage and made a threatening gesture. Then he left his beloved daughter—defeated. A few days later, Saturus baptized Perpetua and the others. After the ceremony, Perpetua sensed God's inviting her to pray for physical stamina to endure any torture that might precede her death.

Soon the six companions were confined in a hellish jail. "I was terrified," said Perpetua, "because I had never experienced such darkness. What a horrible day! Terrible heat because so many were crammed together! Rough treatment by the soldiers! To top it all, I was tormented by anxiety for my baby."

With a bribe, two deacons bought some relief for Perpetua and her friends. They arranged for the transfer of the prisoners to a better part of the jail. Perpetua's mother and brother brought her infant son to her there, and she took great comfort in nursing him again. "I spoke anxiously to my mother about my son," wrote Perpetua, "and encouraged my brother. I commended my son to their care. I was upset because I saw their concern for me."

Somehow the resourceful Perpetua got permission to keep her baby with her, which relieved her worry. "At once," she said, "I recovered my health. My prison suddenly became my palace, and I would rather have been there than anywhere else."

During this calm interlude, Perpetua received a vision that prepared her to face her death courageously. In her mind's eye, she saw a bronze ladder extending into heaven. It was narrow and its sides were lined with hooks, knives, and other sharp tools. So to make the climb, a person had to proceed with great care. A huge serpent lurked at the base of the ladder to terrify people and prevent them from ascending.

In the vision, Saturus, the instructor, climbed the ladder of martyrdom before Perpetua. When he reached the top, he turned to encourage her and to warn her about the serpent. "In the name of Jesus Christ," she heard herself declare, "he will not hurt me." Perpetua made the serpent's head her first step, and it cowered under her foot. Then she climbed the ladder unharmed. Thousands clad in white welcomed her into a beautiful garden. A tall man in shepherd's garb said, "Welcome, child," and gave her deliciously sweet milk curds to eat. When the vision ended, Perpetua felt strengthened in her resolve to die rather than to betray her faith.

In a few days the prisoners, except Secundulus, who had died in jail, were taken to the public square for their trial. The large crowd there snarled curses at them. First the judge interrogated Perpetua's companions, urging them to offer sacrifice. One by one, however, they confessed their faith and refused to comply. When Perpetua's turn came, her fear-crazed father rushed forward. He held her son before her and pleaded with her to reconsider.

"Spare your father," said the judge, "and spare your child. Offer sacrifice for the prosperity of the emperors."

"No," she replied.

"Are you a Christian?"

"Yes."

At this, Perpetua's father tried to pull her away. The judge then had him beaten to stop his interference. Perpetua felt her father's pain as if she herself had been struck, and she was overcome with grief for him. She was also obsessed with fear for her infant, but still she did not change her mind.

The judge ordered that Saturus, Saturninus, and Revocatus be scourged and that Perpetua and Felicity be hit in the face. Then he sentenced them to a fight with wild beasts. Their executions would be the entertainment at a military festival soon to be held in honor of the emperor's birthday. They were returned in chains to prison to await the event.

⟨⟩

Because execution of pregnant women was not allowed, Felicity feared that she might suffer separately from her friends. However, Perpetua and the others prayed for her, and she immediately went into labor. She had a difficult, early delivery. One of the guards taunted Felicity, saying that the beasts would give her much greater pain. "What I am suffering now," she said, "I suffer by myself. But then another inside me will suffer for me, and I for him." She gave birth to a girl, whom Christian friends adopted and raised as their own daughter.

Just before the executions, the Roman tribune ruled that the prisoners could have no visitors. He feared that they might be magically spirited away. But plucky Perpetua confronted him. "Why can't you even allow us a little refreshment?" she asked. "Aren't we the emperor's own distinguished prisoners, since we're going to fight on his birthday? Wouldn't it be to your credit if we were to appear healthy before him at that time?" Her argument got to him, and reddened with embarrassment, he reversed his previous order and allowed visitors.

63

⟨⟩

The night before her death, Perpetua had another reassuring vision. She found herself in the amphitheater but was surprised to discover that she was not facing wild animals. Instead, she was in a hand-to-hand contest with a malicious thug. She saw herself transformed into a mighty warrior ready for battle. Then an extraordinary man appeared, so tall that he towered above the arena. He had the appearance of an athletic trainer. He carried a rod and a branch full of golden apples, and he told her that her foe, if he won, would kill her with a sword. But if Perpetua defeated her foe, the trainer would give her the victory bough.

When Perpetua and her foe began to fight, Perpetua instantly observed that her adversary was doomed. He was no match for her. She was then lifted into the air, as though spiritual forces were assisting her. She thrust her enemy to the ground and crushed his head underfoot. The marvelous presider awarded her the bough, kissed her, and said, "Peace be with you, daughter." She walked triumphantly toward heaven's gate, and the vision ended.

"Thus, I saw that I would not really be fighting with beasts," she said, "but with the devil. But I knew the victory to be mine." After recording this revelation, Perpetua wrote no more. An eyewitness recorded the rest of her story.

The next morning, the guards marched Perpetua and her companions to the arena, where they attempted to force the Christians to wear the robes of Roman priests and priestesses. Perpetua, however, resisted vigorously. "We agreed to pledge our lives," she said, "provided that we would not be made to do this." Because of her fearless intervention, the guards allowed them to enter the amphitheater dressed as they were. As they passed the crowds, Perpetua sang a psalm, and Revocatus, Saturninus, and Saturus shouted at the mob, warning them of God's judgment.

Saturninus and Revocatus died quickly, mauled to death by a leopard and a bear.

Then came Saturus led by Pudens, the soldier who had been in charge of the prisoners in jail. Because of their witness, he had become a Christian. Saturus was afraid of bears and had predicted that he would be quickly killed by a leopard. Things happened just as Saturus had foretold. First he faced a wild boar that did not harm him. However, it gored a soldier, who died within a few days. Then soldiers bound Saturus in stocks as bait for a bear, but the animal refused to leave his cage.

"It is exactly as I predicted," he told Pudens. "So now you may believe me with all your heart. I shall be finished off with one bite of a leopard." And then a leopard was loosed on him. It wounded him mortally, splashing him with blood. "Well washed!" roared the crowd. "Well baptized!" Covered with blood, Saturus said to Pudens, "Remember me, and remember the faith."

As for Perpetua, she never flinched. She seemed completely in control of herself. First, she and Felicity were tossed to the ground by a wild heifer, but Perpetua appeared hardly to notice. After the attack, she sat up and modestly pulled her ripped tunic over her thighs. Then she asked for a pin to fasten her hair in place so as not to appear to be in mourning. Assured that she looked dignified, she rose and helped Felicity to her feet. Together they were taken to one of the arena gates, where Perpetua exhorted her brother and some catechumens: "You must all stand fast in the faith and love one another. And do not be weakened by what we have gone through."

Finally, the soldiers killed the remaining companions by slitting their throats. Before their execution, they greeted each other with a sign of peace. Perpetua shrieked when a nervous young soldier clumsily struck her with his sword. Then she did the unimaginable: she took his shaking hand and guided his weapon to her throat. "It was as though so great a woman," said an eyewitness, "could not be dispatched unless she herself were willing."

65

Perpetua was a passionate lover of people. Her affection for family and friends caused her to be more concerned for them than she was for herself. She loved her father dearly, even though he felt she was treating him cruelly. And she loved her little son tenderly.

Above all, however, Perpetua was a passionate lover of God. Her love for him was a sun whose light subsumed all other loves. Her love for God intensified her love for family and friends. Had she put them ahead of him, I think she would have loved them less.

The Saint's Paradox

Saints are paradoxical characters. They cheerfully endure themselves what they weep to see others endure. . . . They find riches in poverty, happiness in sorrow, and joy in pain. But the children of favor are fathered by a divine paradox: "He who loses his life shall save it" [see Luke 9:24]. . . . They take the paradoxical command literally. And logically enough, with the most paradoxical consequences.

Clare Boothe Luce

Miracles of the Heart

St. Gertrude the Great (1256–1302)

Whatever the expression, everyone is ultimately talking about the same thing—an unquenchable fire, a restlessness, a longing, a disquiet, a hunger, a loneliness, a gnawing nostalgia, a wildness that cannot be tamed, a congenital, all-embracing ache that lies at the center of human experience and is the ultimate force that drives everything else. . . . What we do with our longings, both in terms of handling the pain and the hope they bring us, that is our spirituality.

Ronald Rolheiser

Have you ever looked into your heart and found it empty, hungering for something to fill and comfort it? Have you felt pangs of longing in your soul that cry out for deliverance, courage, freedom—whatever it might take to bring peace? If so, you will identify with St. Gertrude of Helfta, the great thirteenth-century mystic. Originally called "the Great" to distinguish her from other St. Gertrudes, she now bears that title because we appreciate the profundity of her insight into the human condition. She suffered that chaotic hollowness we all sometimes feel, and she found no cure for it until she experienced the healing love of God. Unlike most of us, St. Gertrude enjoyed mystical visions in which Jesus appeared and spoke to her personally. However, while we may never experience a vision of Christ, we can expect him to cure our distressed souls and satisfy our longings just as he did for St. Gertrude.

67

Gertrude arrived at the Benedictine convent in Helfta, Saxony, when she was five years old. We know nothing about her family background but can surmise from clues in her writing that her parents had died, leaving her orphaned. St. Mechtilde, herself a gifted mystic, took Gertrude under her care and over the next two decades supervised her education and Christian formation. By the age of twenty-five, Gertrude had made her profession as a Benedictine nun. She had also become a competent professional scholar who described herself as addicted to the study of secular literature.

In her twenty-sixth year, Gertrude experienced a spiritual crisis that transformed her life. Throughout the month of January 1281, troubled feelings vexed her soul. She does not provide details about her trials, so we do not know what gnawed at her heart. However, the resolution of Gertrude's crisis shows that whatever distressed her, whether some fear, doubt, depression, or other grievous temptation, behind it lurked a desperate longing for God.

On January 27, after night prayers with her sisters, Gertrude went as usual to the dormitory to get ready for bed. As she stood by her cot, Jesus suddenly appeared to her as a handsome young man about sixteen years old. The Lord's friendly demeanor and radiant beauty captivated Gertrude's heart. "Your salvation is right here," he said, touching his breast. "Why are you so sad? Why are you so full of grief?"

As Gertrude tells it in her *Revelations,* when Jesus spoke she was mystically transported to the place where she normally prayed. Addressing him, she writes, "Even though I knew I was standing in the dormitory, it seemed to me that I was in the corner of the choir where I always offered my tepid prayers. And there I heard you say, 'I'll save you. I'll deliver you. Don't be afraid.' After you spoke these words, I saw you put your right hand into mine, as if to ratify your promise.

"Then you said, 'You have licked the dust with my enemies and you have sucked honey from among thorns. But now come back to me. I will receive you and I will inebriate your spirit with a stream of eternal delights.' My soul melted at these tender words. I longed to approach you, but I saw that a huge hedge separated us. It extended so far before and behind me that I couldn't get around it. And jagged thorns covered its top, so that I could find no way to reach you. My body convulsed with tears over my faults and sins, which the hedge that separated us symbolized.

"But you took me by the hand and instantly and easily placed me right beside you. Then I looked at your hand that you had extended to me as a pledge of my salvation and I recognized your radiant wounds that cancelled the claims Satan held against us" (see Colossians 2:14).

This extraordinary moment changed Gertrude forever. She said that afterward she began regularly to experience a closeness to Christ that enabled her to tame her strong-willed, independent spirit. From that time, especially at the reception of the Eucharist, Gertrude sensed the Lord's touch in her heart. She told him that in the Eucharist he not only revealed himself to her more deeply, but he also gave her a clearer self-knowledge, allowing her to correct her faults more out of love than fear. "Now," she said, "I can submit my unconquerable self-opinionatedness to the sweetness of your yoke." From then on she also abandoned the pursuit of literature, which she had loved so dearly, and devoted herself to studying Scripture.

PRAYER ELEVATES THE SOUL
St. Bonaventure (1221–74)

Whenever you call upon God,
Three ideas
Should guide your act of worship:
First, to humble your heart in reverence and adoration of God;
Second, to expand your heart with good will and thanksgiving;
Third, to lift up your heart in delight,
In that converse between lover and Beloved
Taught by the Holy Spirit in the Canticle of Canticles.
If this be done well,
Such wonderful peace and joy result
That they transport the soul from the realm of the senses,
Causing her to say,
"It is good to be here."
Thus should our prayer end,
Until the soul enters into that wonderful tabernacle,
The very house of God,
Where is heard the voice of one rejoicing in exultation.

To be moved to reverence,
Look upon the divine immensity—

69

Then consider yourself,
See your own littleness.
To be filled with good will,
Look upon the benevolence of God
And your own unworthiness.
To be raised unto the union of love,
Remember the charity of God
And your own lukewarmness.
Only by such comparisons
Will you go beyond the things of sense.

About a year after this personal experience of Christ, Gertrude started to pray frequently that he would engrave his wounds on her heart so that she could more fully appreciate his suffering and love. Then one night after vespers, while she was in the refectory enjoying a snack with her sisters, she sensed that the Lord had answered her prayer. "I realized," she told him, "that you had cured my soul by engraving your wounds on it. And you had quenched my spiritual thirst by allowing me to drink of your love."

The impression of Christ's wounds on her heart stayed with Gertrude as a unique form of the stigmata. Daily as she meditated on them, they seemed to purge her of sinfulness and advance her in holiness. However, no marks appeared on her body, and she did not seem to suffer the pain that other stigmatists like Padre Pio endured. Her suffering came instead in the form of serious illnesses that often kept her from participating in the monastery's common life.

Seven years later, Gertrude prayed again that Christ would so wound her heart that his divinity would entirely fill it. Then one day after receiving communion, as she knelt before a crucifix, she perceived a ray of light proceeding like an arrow from Christ's wounded side. It hovered before her until, after Mass, the Lord himself appeared to Gertrude in a vision and gently guided it into her heart. "May the full tide of your affections flow here," he said, "so that my love may sustain all your pleasure, your hope, your joy, your grief, your fear, and every other feeling." After this mysterious event, Gertrude perceived her unity with God to be as complete as the union of the sun's rays with the air that carries them and as intimate as a seal stamped in wax.

Gertrude left us an inspiring and insightful account of her relationship with Christ in her book commonly titled the *Revelations of St. Gertrude.* She wrote only part two of this treatise, and a colleague compiled the remaining four parts. For wisdom on the spiritual life and growth in prayer, *Revelations* compares favorably with the works of St. Teresa of Ávila. Gertrude's confessions about her personal union with the heart of Christ anticipated devotion to the Sacred Heart in later centuries and strongly influenced its development.

Few of us will ever fly the mystical heights with St. Gertrude. If we see visions at all, I suspect they will be of the impenetrable hedge of our thorny sins and faults that keep us from the Lord. However, we should let this great woman remind us that we don't have to muscle our way through our self-constructed blockade. As Jesus did for St. Gertrude, he will lift us over it and instantly bring us to him.

The Gift of Christ's Wounds

Lord, I received from your overflowing liberality this remarkable gift: Each time during the day when I reflected on your adorable wounds, praying the first verses of Psalm 103, I always received some new favor. At verse one, "Bless the Lord, O my soul," I placed all the rust of my sins and sensuousness at the wounds of your blessed feet. At verse two, "Bless the Lord . . . and forget not all his benefits," I washed away all the stains of carnal and perishable pleasures in the sweet bath of blood and water which you poured forth from your side for me. At verse three, "who forgives all your iniquity," I rested my spirit in the wound of your left hand, just as a dove nests in the crevice of the rock. At verse four, "who redeems your life from the

MYSTICS AND MIRACLES

Pit," I took from your right hand all that I needed for my growth in virtue. And so magnificently adorned, I prayed verse five, "who satisfies you with good as long as you live," that I might be purified from all defilement of sin and have the poverty of my wants supplied, so that I might become worthy of your presence and might merit the joy of your holy embraces.

St. Gertrude the Great

72

Wounded Healer

BLESSED PADRE PIO OF PIETRELCINA (1887–1968)

Jesus died on the cross for us, and the entire theology of redemption rests on this truth, one of the principal tenets of our faith. This truth is so important that whenever people have forgotten it or have sought to find it, God has always intervened with events, deeds and miracles. In our time the temptation to forget the reality of the body of Christ is enormous. And God sent this man with the task of calling us back to the truth.

CARDINAL GIUSEPPE SIRI

Critics of Padre Pio of Pietrelcina regarded him as an anomaly, a throwback to earlier times when Christians expected saints to do weird things. "I thought we left such legends back in the Middle Ages," said one incredulous observer. I suspect he had in mind saints like Joseph of Cupertino, who flew through the air at the sight of a statue of Mary. However, Padre Pio's many disciples regarded him as a saint as much for his charity, generosity, and tenderness as for the extraordinary mystical phenomena attributed to him.

Miracles happened every day of Padre Pio's life. Like other wonder-workers such as Francis of Paola, Pio freely contradicted inviolable laws of nature. He appeared in two places at the same time to help people in trouble. He summoned friends by mental telepathy or by causing them to smell the scent of violets, which was associated with his presence. He read people's thoughts and used that special knowledge to tease them. He dumbfounded people in the confessional by describing all their sins in detail. He accurately predicted future events, including his own death. He healed people of deafness, blindness, and incurable diseases. And for fifty years he bore Christ's wounds on his body and suffered enormously because of them.

How do we understand the appearance of such a "medieval" figure in our contemporary world? Perhaps we should not be surprised that God acts dramatically to get our attention when we lose sight of spiritual realities. God sent Padre Pio to us as a light to challenge the darkness of the mid-twentieth century and to offer hope to a world racked by depression and war.

73

In 1903, sixteen-year-old Francesco Forgione entered the Capuchin monastery at Morcone, Italy, where he received the name Brother Pio. A bright young man whose personality blended playfulness and seriousness, he threw himself wholeheartedly into the rigors of the Capuchin novitiate. Perhaps too wholeheartedly, as for the next decade Brother Pio suffered mysterious illnesses that required his superiors to allow him to live with his family in Pietrelcina, his hometown. Inexplicably, the vomiting, fevers, and pains that instantaneously afflicted him when he set foot in the monastery subsided when he returned to his home.

As though determined to nip Pio's ministry in the bud, during these years the devil launched outrageous attacks against him. Almost nightly in his room, the enemy engaged him in violent spiritual and physical battles that left him exhausted and bruised, but not beaten. Before he joined the Capuchins, Pio had received an encouraging vision, similar to the one that had strengthened Perpetua before her martyrdom. In his mind's eye he watched himself conquer a huge, hideous monster. A beautiful youth assisted Pio and prophetically acknowledged his victory by placing a glittering crown on his head with a promise of even greater conquests to come. Frequent contests with the devil over the years made Pio an adept spiritual warrior.

In 1910, he became Padre Pio when the Capuchins ordained him a priest. He conducted his early pastoral ministry in Pietrelcina because his baffling illnesses recurred every time his superiors tried to return him to a monastery. Padre Pio celebrated Mass in the morning at his parish church and spent his days praying, teaching children, counseling people, and visiting friends. Impressed by his obvious piety and touched by his gentle affection, the people of Pietrelcina soon came to esteem their young priest as a saint.

Miracles and mystical phenomena fueled Padre Pio's reputation for holiness. Perhaps his earliest miracle occurred during this time at

Pietrelcina. Once, he sent his favorite aunt, Daria, a bag of chestnuts, which she ate. Shortly afterward she tripped while rummaging in a dark shed. Her oil lamp ignited gunpowder that her husband had stored there, and the explosion knocked her down and severely burned her face. Daria ran to the house and covered her face with the bag Pio had sent. Immediately her pain stopped, and every trace of the burn disappeared.

Pio worked another miracle on behalf of the welfare of the whole town. In the spring of 1913, an infestation of lice threatened to destroy Pietrelcina's entire bean crop. The insects covered plants of all of the town's farms. One farmer invited Padre Pio to pray for his crop, and as he interceded, the lice noisily popped off the plants. Then he went to all the other farms, clearing out the lice field-by-field with his prayer. When the town harvested an especially abundant bean crop that year, they celebrated their saint again.

Such events confirmed the people of Pietrelcina's belief that a saint lived among them. Padre Pio's Mass could last as long as three hours, which parishioners tolerated because they considered him a saint. During his long thanksgivings after Mass, he often fell to the floor, unconscious, his body going rigid while he slipped into ecstasy. Once, the sacristan thought Padre Pio had died when he found him passed out in the sanctuary three hours after Mass. He ran to the pastor, shouting, "The monk is dead!" The pastor, who realized what was going on, calmed him down. "Don't worry," he said. "He'll come to."

In the summer of 1916, Padre Pio visited the friary of Our Lady of Grace near the village of San Giovanni Rotondo in the Gargano Mountains. He fell in love with the poor monastery and sensed that the Lord wanted him to dwell there. At Pio's request, the Capuchins permanently assigned him in 1917 to Our Lady of Grace, where he would live for the rest of his life.

A significant miracle touched Padre Pio when he moved to San Giovanni Rotondo, one that sometimes goes unnoticed: the Lord instantly healed him of the strange illnesses that had dogged him for ten years every time he had attempted to stay at other monasteries.

Perhaps God had allowed the mysterious sicknesses as a way of bringing Padre Pio to his destined place of service. For during the next fifty years, Padre Pio's ministry transformed the isolated monastery at San Giovanni Rotondo into a world-renowned spiritual renewal center.

A series of mystical events that occurred in August and September of 1918 shaped the remainder of Padre Pio's life. On August 5, an angel like the one who struck Teresa of Ávila's heart appeared to him and wounded his soul. Later he described to his spiritual director what had happened: "I was filled with extreme terror at the sight of a heavenly Being who presented himself to the eye of my intellect. In his hand he held some kind of weapon, like a long, sharp-pointed steel blade, which seemed to spew out fire. He hurled this weapon into my soul with all his might. It was only with difficulty that I did not cry out. I thought I was dying. . . . This agony lasted until the morning of August 7. . . . Even my internal organs were torn and ruptured by that weapon. Since that day I have been mortally wounded. I always feel in the depths of my soul a wound that is always open and that causes me continual agony."

Then after celebrating Mass on September 18, while sitting in the monastery choir before an ancient crucifix, Padre Pio received the stigmata. He says he fell into a deep, peaceful repose, and an angel with blood oozing from his hands, feet, and side appeared to him. "I felt like I was dying," he said, "and I would have died if the Lord had not intervened to strengthen my heart, which was ready to burst out of my chest. When the mysterious creature left, I found that my hands, feet, and side had been pierced and were bleeding. . . . The wound in my heart bleeds continuously, especially from Thursday evening until Saturday. I'm afraid that I will bleed to death if the Lord doesn't hear my groans and take these wounds from me. He can even leave the anguish and the pain, but let him take away these visible signs that are a source of embarrassment for me and an indescribable and unbearable humiliation."

For his own good reasons, the Lord said no to Padre Pio's prayer. But his no was a yes to the many people whose lives were touched by the miracles that flowed from Padre Pio's wounded hands during the next half-century.

~

Of thousands of miracles that reportedly came through Padre Pio, the most celebrated and interesting wonders occurred through his involvement with the Marchioness Giovanna Rizzani Boschi, one of his dedicated spiritual daughters.

On January 18, 1905, while Pio, then a young monk, was praying at the monastery of St. Elia in Piansi, he was miraculously transported to the garden of a mansion in the Udine. Giovanni Battista Rizzani, the father of the family, was on his deathbed, and Leonilde, the mother, was about to give birth to Giovanna. Leonilde went outside to quiet the howling of the master's dogs, and there, in the garden, she went into labor and delivered her baby. Whenever Leonilde reminisced about that memorable day, she always said that she had seen a young Capuchin at Giovanna's birth. And Brother Pio reported to his spiritual director that he had mysteriously witnessed the birth. He also said that before he found himself back at the monastery, the Virgin Mary had appeared to him in the Rizzani garden. She had entrusted Giovanna to him as a diamond in the rough and had instructed him to polish her until she shone beautifully. "She will seek you out," said Mary, "but first you will meet her in St. Peter's."

Seventeen years later, Giovanna, full of doubts about her faith, went to St. Peter's Basilica looking for a priest who might help her. A sacristan told her that the basilica was about to close and no priests were available, but a Capuchin seemed to appear from nowhere. He welcomed her into his confessional and provided satisfying answers to some of the questions that bedeviled her. Afterward Giovanna waited outside to greet the priest, but he never came out, having disappeared as quietly as he had arrived.

One day during the following summer, she learned about Padre Pio, and a few days later she followed a compelling desire to seek him out at San Giovanni Rotondo. At the monastery, she stood in a crowd hoping to see him. As he walked by, he stopped in front of her and startled her by saying, "Giovanna, I know you. You were born the day your father died." Then he walked away.

The next morning a perplexed Giovanna went to Padre Pio for confession. "Daughter," he said, "at last you have come to me. I have been waiting for you for a long time."

"Father, you must be mistaken," said Giovanna. "This is my first time at San Giovanni Rotondo. I never knew you existed until a few days ago."

"No, I am making no mistake," he said. "Last summer at St. Peter's you asked a Capuchin priest to help you with your doubts about your faith. I was that priest."

Then Giovanna recognized him. Her heart beat with excitement as he continued his story.

"When you were being born, the Virgin Mary took me to your home. I witnessed your birth in the garden. Mary entrusted you to my care and made me responsible to help you grow in holiness. She told me that someday I would meet you at St. Peter's."

These revelations touched Giovanna dramatically, and she became one of Padre Pio's spiritual daughters. A few years later he had her join the Franciscan Third Order. Customarily, new members of the order had to choose a new name, and Padre Pio gave her the unusual name Jacoba.

"What an ugly name," said Giovanna. "I don't like it."

"You will be called Sister Jacoba," he explained, "because like Jacoba, the noble Roman friend who was present at the death of St. Francis, you will be present at my death."

Giovanna remembered that strange prediction in September of 1968, when she was visiting Padre Pio at Our Lady of Grace. In the early morning of September 23, she had a vision in which she was transported to Padre Pio's cell, where she witnessed his death. Later when she told one of the monks about it, she accurately

78

described his cell, which she had never visited, and named those who had attended him in his final hour.

As he did with Giovanna, Padre Pio always used his exceptional gifts to advance people in their relationship with God. His interventions in the lives of others produced remarkable and durable conversions. Unbelievers, atheists, agnostics, lapsed and lukewarm Catholics—he turned all to the Lord with a word of revelation or a healing.

Let the case of Alberto Del Fante stand for hundreds of others. Del Fante, a journalist, despised Padre Pio. He denounced him in magazines as a charlatan who preyed on gullible people. A few years later his beloved grandson, Enrico, was afflicted with kidney disease and tuberculosis, and physicians offered little hope for the boy's recovery. Relatives went to Our Lady of Grace to ask Padre Pio to pray for Enrico. They returned and told Del Fante of Padre Pio's assurance that the boy would recover. "If Enrico gets well," he promised, "I will make a pilgrimage to San Giovanni Rotondo myself." He was sure that nothing would happen, but Enrico was healed. Touched deeply by the child's miraculous cure, Del Fante went to Our Lady of Grace, where Padre Pio helped him turn to God. After Del Fante's conversion experience, he became a dedicated promoter of Padre Pio and his ministry.

Padre Pio struggled all his life with irritability, a problem that long hours in the confessional and short hours of sleep intensified. But he redeemed this fault by putting it to good use. He employed his brusque demeanor to prod people to confront honestly the condition of their souls. Once, he loudly chased a famous actress from his confessional. He refused to hear her confession because he had discerned that she had not faced up to her sinfulness. "He's anything but holy," she said to a friend. "He's rude and ill-mannered. I never want to see him again." However, she could not get him out of her mind. "Padre Pio is pursuing me," she said. "I feel like I will never be peaceful again until I speak with him." The actress returned to Our Lady of

Grace, and this time Padre Pio received her graciously because she was now focused on her relationship with God. In this way he used his famous gruffness as an evangelistic tool.

Padre Pio also used his edgy toughness as a means of controlling his feelings. Once, for example, a woman carried a wicker suitcase into his confessional. With loud sobs and shrieks, she opened it to show him her six-month-old son, who had died on the way to San Giovanni Rotondo. Padre Pio gently lifted the tiny body into his arms and prayed briefly. Then he growled at the mother, "Why are you yelling so much? Don't you see that your son is sleeping?" When the baby returned to life, Padre Pio had to fight back tears of joy. He said that he resorted to toughness in situations like this to prevent himself from being overwhelmed by his tender emotions.

Focusing too much on Padre Pio's marvels and mystical phenomena gives the false impression that he led an abnormal life, more angelic than human. While he opened our eyes to heavenly realities, he kept his feet firmly planted on the earth, enduring and enjoying ordinary things, as other human beings did. Today we mainly imagine him as a wonder-working stigmatic with miracles flowing from his wounded hands. But the people who knew him, while they appreciated his marvels, loved him more for his earthiness, his compassion, his gentleness, his humor, and his common sense. For instance, when he was asked his opinion of a thief who had stolen valuable gems from a church's painting of the Virgin, he responded, "What do you want me to say? That poor young man was probably hungry and went to Our Lady to say: 'Of what use are these jewels to you?' And probably Our Lady gave them to him. Silly him to get caught with the goods in his pocket."

Padre Pio embraced his own great suffering as his personal share in the suffering of Christ. But he could not endure the suffering of others. Hundreds came to Our Lady of Grace hoping for a healing, and he knew that only some of them would receive a miraculous cure.

His compassion for the many who would not be healed led him to work for the establishment of a world-class hospital at San Giovanni Rotondo that would serve the poor. From the outset he planned to name it "House for the Relief of Suffering."

Padre Pio worked against all odds to achieve his goal of creating a medical center. He faced obstacles that would have deflated the enthusiasm of lesser men. How does a monk vowed to poverty build a hospital without any money in an impoverished town situated on an inaccessible mountain? Padre Pio did it by faith and with a small army of friends. His associates helped him raise money, design and construct the buildings, and assemble a top-shelf medical staff. When the House for the Relief of Suffering opened in 1956, many observers believed it could not survive because of its location on a desolate mountain. However, Padre Pio believed otherwise. When he inaugurated the first building, he said, "Now House for the Relief of Suffering is a small seed, but it will become a mighty oak, a hospital that is a small city and a center for clinical studies of international importance." That prophecy has come true. Today the hospital is a thriving center whose expanding complex resembles a little city.

Padre Pio's practical compassion and entrepreneurial genius defy those who might be tempted to dismiss him as a medieval weirdo. Instead he stands for all as a modern icon of God's inexhaustible love for human beings and his determination to rescue us at all costs.

Make Your Father Proud

Live in such a way that your heavenly Father may be proud of you, as he is proud of so many other chosen souls. Live in such a way that you may be able to repeat at every moment with the apostle St. Paul: Be imitators of me, as I am of Jesus Christ [see 1 Corinthians 11:1]. Oh, for pity's sake, do not consider this an exaggeration! Every Christian who is a true imitator and follower of the Nazarene can and must call himself a second Christ and show forth most clearly in his life the entire image of Christ. Oh, if only all Christians were to live up to their vocation, this very land of exile would be changed into a paradise.

Padre Pio

PART FOUR

MIRACLES *of* CONVERSION

Go into all the world and preach the good news to all creation. Whoever believes and is baptized will be saved, but whoever does not believe will be condemned. And these signs will accompany those who believe: In my name they will drive out demons; they will speak in new tongues; they will pick up snakes with their hands; and when they drink deadly poison, it will not hurt them at all; they will place their hands on sick people, and they will get well.

MARK 16:15–18

hrist's first public miracle was one of conversion. At the wedding at Cana, he converted water into wine because his mother asked him to (see John 2:1–11). Among my favorite persons in the Bible are those unnamed waiters who did what Jesus told them to do and lugged six huge water jars over to him. I admire them because by simply following Christ's directions they became collaborators in a remarkable wonder. Those servants seem to me to be prototypes of the mystics from whose obedience miracles also flowed.

Perhaps the conversion of water to wine hinted at another more fundamental Christian miracle of conversion, the transformation of human beings into children of God. Again, I think that conversion also points to the mystics. Exemplars of conversion themselves, they were dedicated to helping others enter the Christian miracle and become transformed in Christ. The miracle of personal conversion lies at the heart of Christianity. It sums up what Christians call the "Good News." This miracle, in fact, is the message.

Through the ages, the mystics' exemplary lives have broadcast the Christian promise of conversion. The relentless generosity of mystics like Martin and Elizabeth showed the world that it had been touched by God. The mystics' unremitting kindness defies mere human explanations. Their unselfish goodness so repels our natural selfishness that we must suspect it has a divine source. No one can be that good all the time on his or her own strength. The miracles that poured forth from the mystics' charity confirmed that a supernatural impulse quickened them. Thus, the miracle of their lives is their message.

The example of the martyrs is an even more convincing testimony to the Christian gospel. Observers had to be moved by the courage of saints like Apphian and Sabas. They had to be curious about these young men who embraced death so willingly. How could they freely choose the thing most repugnant to human beings? Were Apphian and Sabas touched by madness or by God? Onlookers must have toyed with this question. The miracles that attended their martyrdom argued in favor of a divine touch.

Mystics who were preachers or teachers played a special role in communicating the Christian message of conversion. Some, like Anthony of Padua, were gifted with dynamic eloquence. A medieval forerunner of Billy Graham, he attracted and swayed thousands wherever he went. Some mystics, like Dominic, were strategic speakers. He not only dazzled crowds by confronting and confuting heretics, but he also multiplied his influence by training a band of gifted men in his style and methods. Visions and dreams guided both Dominic and Anthony, and miracles authenticated their preaching. They were major players in the extraordinary spiritual renewal of the thirteenth century, and their arrival on that scene seems in itself miraculous.

And then there's Vincent Ferrer, who may be in a class all by himself. Preacher, diplomat, visionary, healer, wonder-worker—you name it, he seems to have done it all. Simply put, Vincent Ferrer's life was a continuous miracle of conversion. If you are familiar with him, you know what I mean. If you are not, you will get to know him in the following pages.

Miracles of conversion like the one at Cana and the lives of saints give me hope. They convince me that Christ can transform the likes of me.

Miracles in Action
St. Dominic (1170–1221)

In the presence of a significant life, we behold not only our own life as it is but possibilities and potential for the future.

Anthony Padovano

St. Dominic was a carefully crafted arrow strategically aimed at the thirteenth century. "Carefully crafted" because his education and training specifically prepared him for a life's work he did not anticipate. "Strategically aimed" because he struck at the heart of problems afflicting the church and the world of his day. And history shows that he was right on target.

Joan of Aza, Dominic's mother, was a remarkable woman on her own account. Later beatified by the Roman Catholic Church, she had several visions that predicted her son's significant work. Before Dominic was born, she dreamed that she would bear a son who would be a shining light to the church. During her pregnancy, Joan also dreamed that she bore a dog in her womb and that it broke away from her, carrying in its mouth a burning torch by which it set fire to the world.

Dominic was born in 1170 at Caleruega in Castile. Just before his baptism, Joan had a third prophetic dream. On her baby's forehead appeared a bright star that enlightened the world. Granted, many mothers have big dreams for their infants. Mostly, however, these are merely hopes that may or may not be realized. But Joan's dreams were revelations that came true.

When Dominic was seven, Joan sent him to study with his uncle, the parish priest at Gumiel d'Izan. At fourteen, he enrolled in the University of Palencia. There, Dominic completed his secular studies within six years. Then he devoted four years to the study of theology.

Jordan of Saxony, the saint's first biographer, tells us that during these years Dominic immersed himself in Scripture. He studied it thoroughly, diligently recording his teacher's insights in the margins of his parchment copy of the Bible.

For Dominic, however, acting on Scripture was more important than studying it. In 1195, Spain was ravaged by war and famine, and impoverished refugees poured into Palencia. Moved by their plight, Dominic sold all his possessions in order to contribute to their relief. He even sold his precious parchments. "I will not study on dead skins," he said, "when others are dying of hunger."

Dominic's generous example caught the attention of Diego d'Azevedo, the prior of the chapter at Osma. A chapter was a religious community of men, usually located at a cathedral church. Its members were called "canons" because they lived according to a rule, or canon. Diego was recruiting talented young men for his diocese, and he had his bishop invite Dominic to join his community of clerics. Thus in 1195, at age twenty-five, Dominic became a canon of the cathedral at Osma. Within the year he was ordained a priest.

Diego's community had adopted the Rule of St. Augustine, which incorporated many features of early Christian piety. Daily observance of that life pattern for nine years completed Dominic's formation. At Osma, he mastered the spiritual disciplines of prayer and self-denial. Dominic prayed for many hours each day, sometimes long into the night. He was often observed weeping for sinners and for the afflicted. Jordan said that Dominic "was persuaded that he could not truly be a member of Christ unless he consecrated himself wholly to the work of gaining souls." It would not be long before Dominic got his heart's desire.

Diego became bishop of Osma in 1201, and Dominic succeeded him as prior of the chapter. Three years later, King Alphonsus IX of Castile sent Bishop Diego to Denmark to arrange a marriage for his son. Diego took Dominic along as his companion. That mission occasioned a major shift in his life from a predominantly contemplative phase to a predominantly active one.

⌒

Their journey took Diego and Dominic through Languedoc, a stronghold of the Albigensians, a sect that had won many converts in southern France and northern Italy. In contrast to a somewhat decadent Christian clergy, the Albigensian leaders seemed to be paragons of virtue. People were attracted to their rigorously simple lifestyle. Rooted in ancient Eastern religions, Albigensianism proclaimed a stark dualism, holding that everything material is evil and everything spiritual is good. They denied the humanity of Christ because they believed that a wicked body could not contain God's pure spirit. Their prohibition of all procreation and their endorsement of suicide threatened ordinary society.

When the party stopped at Toulouse, Dominic stayed at an inn with an Albigensian host. He spent the night persuading the man that his beliefs were false. The next morning, the innkeeper renounced his errors and returned to the Christian faith. That event foreshadowed Dominic's future service, as he seemed ideally equipped to help turn the Albigensian tide. Dominic himself did not see it at first. Pursuing their dream of Christianizing the Tartars, he and Diego continued on to Rome to ask Pope Innocent III's leave to preach the gospel in Russia. But the pope had other ideas. He charged them to return to Languedoc to assist in the recovery of Christians who had fallen prey to the Albigensians.

89

⌒

Back in France, Dominic and Diego confirmed their suspicions about the failure of efforts against the heresy. Dominic observed that the clergy leading the campaign appeared lax and wealthy. They were no match for the austere sect leaders. He recommended that all preachers win the right to be heard by imitating the self-denial of their opponents. He also believed that gentle persuasion rather than vigorous condemnation was the way to bring Albigensians back to the Christian faith.

In 1206, Dominic and Diego engaged in a series of disputations with Albigensian leaders. The most memorable of these was held at Fanjeux in Languedoc, where both sides agreed to accept the decision of a panel of lay judges. Each group prepared a written summary of its strongest arguments. Dominic prepared the church's case. After reviewing the presentations, the judges refused to decide. Instead, they demanded a trial by fire, a not-unusual practice at the time.

An official threw the documents, one at a time, into a great bonfire. The Albigensian case was first. The onlookers watched in stony silence as the flames hungrily consumed it. But Dominic's book was mysteriously thrust out of the flames intact. "Hurrah!" someone shouted, and the astonished crowd began to cheer. Not satisfied with the result, the judges repeated the trial. Once again the official submitted copies of both documents to the blaze. It was a repeat performance—the Albigensian book was reduced to ashes, and Dominic's emerged unharmed. Greatly entertained by this wonder, the crowd hooted its approval. Even though Dominic had already won the best out of three, the judges ran the test again. A third time, Dominic's book triumphed. The onlookers guffawed, and some of them sniped jokes at the Albigensians. This triple miracle, however, did not convince Dominic's opponents. They reneged on the agreement to accept the judges' decision and suppressed news of the wonder.

Such debates accomplished little in the battle against the Albigensians. Dominic would achieve much more through the creation of his communities of men and women. By their word and example these dedicated believers would change hearts throughout Europe.

Dominic conceived a plan to raise up counterorganizations against the highly structured sect. In contrast to the heretics, the church appeared to him to be in disarray. He decided that since people seemed attracted to the community life of the Albigensians, the church must create similar communities that would draw them back. Perhaps the idea first came to him when he observed the success of the sect's well-organized schools, which the heretics used to recruit young women. As an alternative, Dominic wanted to establish a sisterhood of Catholic women who could offer a safe education for girls.

One night in July 1206, Dominic was resting on a hill near Fanjeux overlooking the little village of Prouille. He enjoyed the cool breeze that rustled the leaves and refreshed him with the fragrance of the grass and summer flowers. Gazing at the moonlit houses all quieted for the night, he drifted into prayer. As he watched, a fiery globe seemed to descend from the heavens and rest over a chapel dedicated to Mary. Dominic interpreted this vision as a sign from God that he was to establish a community of women at the church of Our Lady of Prouille.

Dominic's first sisters were nine former Albigensians who were converted by his preaching. He provided them a simple rule of life and charged them to run a school for girls. He also directed them to pray for his work of preaching. On December 27, 1206, the women took up residence at the Prouille church.

Nearby, Dominic opened a house for his associates, men carefully chosen for their gifts and specially trained as preachers. Thus Dominic laid the groundwork for what would become his gift to the church—religious communities that would revolutionize the world through prayer, preaching, and education.

At Rome in 1215, Dominic sought Pope Innocent III's official approval for his projects. The pope readily authorized the Prouille sisterhood, but he was reluctant to give approval to the Friars Preachers because the bishops at the Fourth Lateran Council had recently ruled against the multiplication of new religious orders. Then, in a dream, the pope saw Dominic holding up the collapsing basilica of St. John Lateran. Moved by the vision, he encouraged Dominic to dodge the council's decision by choosing an existing religious rule for his brothers. In August 1216, Dominic and sixteen associates met at Prouille and adopted the Rule of St. Augustine. The following October, Dominic returned to Rome, where Pope Honorius III, Innocent's successor, gave final approval for the Friars Preachers.

It is said that while in Rome, Dominic had a vision in which Mary showed Jesus two figures whose work would spare the world from

God's wrath. He recognized himself as one. In church the next day, he identified an unkempt beggar as the other. He embraced Francis of Assisi and said, "You are my companion. You must walk with me." So the two great men became friends.

On August 13, 1217, Dominic met with his friars at Prouille. He instructed them in his methods of preaching, exhorting them to put a priority on holiness and on study. He also spoke about humility, faith, endurance, and spiritual warfare. Then, two days later, to the surprise of all, Dominic divided his little community, dispersing brothers all over Europe. "Leave it to me," he said. "I know what I'm about. We must sow the seed, not hoard it." Seven brothers went to Paris, four to Spain, two to Toulouse, and two remained at Prouille. Dominic and a companion returned to Rome, where he hoped at last to get the pope's permission to evangelize the Tartars. But it was not to be.

At Rome, the pope commissioned Dominic to establish a group of friars at the church of St. Sixtus. The pope also assigned him to conduct a reformation among certain nuns scattered throughout Rome who were living without much supervision. While he was about these tasks, two famous miracles occurred.

The Rome foundation of Friars Preachers grew quickly. By 1219, about forty men resided at St. Sixtus. One day when there was no food in the house, two brothers were sent to beg. Near the end of the day, all they had received was one loaf of bread. When a beggar approached them for alms, the friars gave it to him. They returned home empty-handed. When Dominic heard their report, he said, "It was an angel of the Lord. The Lord knows how to provide for his own. Let's go and pray." Dominic prayed briefly in the church, then with the brothers in the refectory. After Dominic blessed the friars, two handsome young men appeared. They carried bread in two white cloths that hung from their shoulders. Beginning at the lowest table and ending with Dominic, they distributed a loaf to each brother. Then, just as mysteriously as they had arrived, they disappeared. Dominican houses still commemorate this miracle daily; food is distributed first to the lay brothers and then to the priests, from the youngest to the most senior.

By Lent 1219, with grace and diplomacy, Dominic had persuaded forty-four sisters in Rome to unite in one community. He gave the nuns St. Sixtus, and the pope assigned him a new center for the friars. Dominic and three cardinals received the sisters' profession on Ash Wednesday. During the ceremony, word came that Napoleon, a nephew of one of the cardinals, had fallen from his horse and died.

Dominic had the corpse carried into the chapel. Then he assembled the cardinals, nuns, and friars and celebrated Mass. When he finished, he stood over Napoleon's broken body and straightened his limbs. Dominic blessed the corpse, and with his hands raised to heaven, he shouted, "Napoleon, in the name of our Lord Jesus Christ, arise." Immediately, in view of many reliable witnesses, the young man arose, sound and whole. Amazed and delighted, the cardinals and many others embraced him affectionately.

93

During these years, Dominic visited friaries throughout Europe. He had been right about scattering the seed. By 1221, when he died, he had sixty friaries that were divided into eight provinces. The Friars Preachers were established, at that time, in France, Italy, Spain, and England and had gone to Poland, Scandinavia, and the Holy Land.

For a long time I have believed that spiritual health depends on paying attention to a few essentials. Spending daily time in prayer. Studying regularly. Participating in a community. Reaching out to others. I struggle to make these activities part of my own life. I look back and realize that too often I have neglected one or another of them. St. Dominic, on the other hand, practiced all these essentials until they became second nature to him. Perhaps that's why he could respond so readily and effectively to God's call. As I reflect on his life, my hope is revived that even in my late middle age I can acquire the spiritual disciplines. I'm smart enough to know that all the hard work in the world won't "earn" me God's touch. If the Holy Spirit is going to strike, I want to be a ready target. Prayer, study, and the like can put me right on the bull's-eye.

On Self-Control

A person who governs his passions is master of the world. We must either rule them, or be ruled by them. It is better to be the hammer than the anvil.

St. Dominic

Miracles in Death

St. Sabas and St. Apphian (fourth century)

What saint has ever won his crown without first contending for it?

St. Jerome

Christianity spread throughout the world by word and by deed and especially by the example of martyrs.

Personally, I am particularly moved by young martyrs like St. Perpetua, who had convincing reasons to live—families, babies, position, wealth, comforts. The same was true of St. Sabas and St. Apphian. They were twenty year olds with their whole lives ahead of them. Yet they abandoned it all, and their deaths proclaimed their faith to everyone they left behind. And the miracles that occurred in the wake of their deaths affirmed the message of these youthful martyrs.

⌒

We know little about St. Sabas's life. However, we have a detailed account of his martyrdom and of the miracles surrounding his death.

In the mid-fourth century, marauding Goths made occasional raids into Asia Minor. They captured Christians there and brought them back as slaves to their bases in the northeastern Roman Empire. The captives soon converted some of their masters, and Christian communities developed among the Goths. In 370, a Gothic commander launched a persecution of Christians in his region. Over several years, fifty-one Goths were martyred. Sabas was the most famous of these.

Sabas converted to Christianity as a boy and served the church as cantor for a priest named Sansala. During the persecution, the magistrates ordered Christians to eat meat offered to pagan gods, a practice the church condemned as idolatry. Some pagan Goths tried to protect their Christian relatives with a subterfuge, secretly arranging for them to be served meat that had not been sacrificed.

Sabas, however, would have none of this trickery. Not only did he repudiate the ruse by refusing to eat at all, but he also publicly rebuked those who submitted to it as having betrayed Christ. Although the persecutors ignored Sabas this time, he caught their attention again the following year. To defend family and friends, some leaders of his town gathered before an imperial official to swear falsely that no Christians lived there. Sabas boldly interrupted the proceedings. "Let no one swear for me!" he shouted. "I am a Christian." Once again he escaped punishment because the official judged that the poor young man was not influential enough to cause any real harm.

In a short time the persecution escalated. Just after Easter, Atharidus, a Gothic commander, and his soldiers came to town. One night they broke into Sansala and Sabas's house and carried the priest off in a cart. After beating Sabas with clubs, they dragged his naked body over thorn bushes. The ardent youth may have received this special treatment because he had not shown the soldiers much respect.

The next morning the brash saint taunted his torturers. "Didn't you drag me naked over thorns? Check me over! Look and see if my feet are wounded. See if your blows left any bruises on my body." They examined him and found not a mark, as Sabas had either been protected or miraculously healed.

Furious, the soldiers decided to make Sabas suffer all the more. They transformed a cart into a makeshift rack and tortured him for the better part of a night. A female companion of the soldiers gave him a chance to escape, but he refused to leave. The next day the soldiers hung him from a beam by his hands. When they tired of abusing him, they offered him some meat that had been sacrificed to their gods. "This meat," said Sabas, "is as impure and profane as Atharidus who sent it!"

An infuriated soldier thrust his javelin at Sabas's chest. Everyone thought that he must be dead, but the young man was not even hurt. He jeered his attacker. "Did you think you killed me? Your javelin felt as soft as a skein of wool!" Although Sabas was spared once again by a miraculous reprieve, he would not be denied his chance at martyrdom.

When word of these events reached Atharidus, he sentenced Sabas to death by drowning. At the riverside, one of the officials charged with the execution proposed that they let the young man go. "Sabas is innocent," he said, "and Atharidus need never know."

But Sabas rebuked the man and urged him to follow orders. "I can see what you cannot see," he said. "I see the people on the opposite side of the river who are ready to receive my soul and conduct me to glory. They are only waiting for the moment when it leaves my body."

The executioners then rigged a plank over Sabas's shoulders and held him under water with the board until he drowned.

Witnesses to such a death must have pondered two questions: "Why?" and "What?" *Why* had Sabas suppressed his natural survival instinct? *Why* would anyone choose to die? *What* made Sabas do it? *What* was in it for him? In their puzzlement, perhaps they thought he gave his life because he was convinced he was going to a better place. Or they may have perceived that Sabas died because he believed in something worth more than life itself. But they wouldn't have begun to penetrate the mystery of this man's death until they posed the most important question of all: "Who?" *Who* had so captivated Sabas's heart that he was willing to be murdered for his sake? The answer, of course, is Christ—the one who was murdered for Sabas's sake.

97

Like St. Sabas, St. Apphian was killed by drowning. However, his death was more dramatic because of the miracle that it occasioned.

Apphian was a twenty-year-old youth who lived in Caesarea in the home of Eusebius, the historian. In his book *The Martyrs of Palestine,* Eusebius gave a firsthand account of Apphian's courageous martyrdom and of a miracle that occurred at his death.

In 303, the emperor Galerius launched a general persecution of Christians by decreeing that everyone must participate in public sacrifices. Apphian, his youthful idealism enhanced by his faith, decided to oppose the local enforcement of the decree. Eusebius says the young man confided his plan to no one, "not even to us."

Apphian sneaked past the guards to the spot where Urban, the governor of Caesarea, was offering the sacrifice. He restrained the governor by grabbing his arm. "We must not do this!" he shouted to the crowd. "Worshiping these lifeless gods is wicked! It will be our doom!"

Eusebius reported that the guards seized Apphian and beat him until his face was unrecognizable. Then they locked his feet in stocks and confined him to a dungeon. Twenty-four hours later the guards brought the young man out and tortured him. They tore his sides, exposing his bones and entrails, but the brave youth persevered. When asked a question, the young man simply replied, "I am a servant of Christ!"

The soldiers lit oil-soaked pieces of flax and held them to his feet. Apphian did not falter even when the fire burnt his flesh to the bone. His torturers promised relief only if he would offer the pagan sacrifice. "I confess Christ," he said, "the one God, and the same God with the Father." Because Apphian resolutely refused to comply, the magistrate ordered that he be drowned, a sentence the frustrated guards were delighted to carry out. They weighted down Apphian's feet with heavy stones, and with derisive laughter and triumphant shouts they cast him into the sea.

Eusebius says that the entire population witnessed the miracle that occurred upon the young saint's death. A violent earthquake shook both the city and the sea. Then, stones and all, the body of the martyr was hurled out of the water and onto the shore.

Apphian's fearless death and the subsequent miracle must have made the people of Caesarea think twice about what they had done. His witness gives me some second thoughts, too. Apphian loved God so passionately that he adamantly refused to accommodate himself to anything he saw as evil. Nothing, not even the fear of death, could move him to betray the one he loved above all. Apphian's radicalism challenges my mediocrity and makes me ask dangerous questions.

How passionately do I love God? What are my true priorities? Does material comfort mean more to me than spiritual reality? Would a little pain or humiliation be enough to swerve me off course? Do I accommodate evil because I am afraid of the consequences? I'd better watch out. Questions like these cut deep.

Being on Purpose

Put Christ first, because he put us first, and let nothing deter us from loving him.

St. Cyprian of Carthage

Miracles in His Mouth

ST. ANTHONY OF PADUA (1195–1231)

Society, wounded with the sores of evil, is Lazarus. We are the dogs who must draw near to cure with our tongues—our preaching—by which we lick with the milk and honey of kindness and gentleness, healing not aggravating the evils that afflict humankind.

ST. ANTHONY OF PADUA

Had you passed Anthony of Padua on the street, you might not have noticed him. If you had, you would not have been impressed. Short, swarthy, and pudgy, he was quiet and reserved—hardly the life of any party.

Had you heard him preach, however, you would have been mesmerized. His sonorous voice would have captured you and held you fast. Like many others in the crowd, you would have been certain he was speaking directly to you. His message might have made you angry. You might have brushed away tears of remorse or felt compelled to action. Whatever your response, you would never have forgotten this Anthony of Padua.

He was a dynamic speaker encased in a reticent person. That is not as paradoxical as it might seem. Anthony's reserve was a shell for a core of strength, and fortitude was his outstanding quality. He fearlessly confronted crowds and individuals, even exalted ones such as princes and bishops. Anthony's character was just the right container for his remarkable charisma, and his preaching was a divine endowment, a supernatural gift.

Anthony had signs and wonders in his preacher's portfolio. But his most significant miracles were subtle, invisible ones that changed people's lives. "Preaching," said Anthony, "is a pen which should write faith and virtue in the hearts of the hearers."

Born in Lisbon, Portugal, in 1195, Anthony spent his adult life working in Italy and France. His given name was Ferdinand de Bulhões, but he took the name Anthony when he entered the Friars Minor, the religious order started by St. Francis of Assisi. Eventually, he became known as Anthony of Padua because he spent his last five years in that Italian city.

Young Ferdinand was serious, studious, and spiritual. His parents entrusted his early schooling to the priests at the Lisbon cathedral. In 1210, at the age of fifteen, Ferdinand entered the regular canons of St. Augustine, who had a monastery just outside the city. Because rowdy friends pestered him with frequent visits, Ferdinand was transferred to a house at Coimbra two years later. There he spent eight quiet years of prayer and study. With his prodigious memory, he acquired an extensive knowledge of Scripture, which he would use later in his preaching.

In 1220, the remains of five Franciscans who had been martyred in Morocco were brought to Coimbra. The event fired Ferdinand's desire to give his life for Christ. Since the Augustinian community provided no opportunity for dangerous mission work, he decided to make a change. The next year he joined the Friars Minor on the condition that he would be sent to serve in Morocco. When he left Coimbra, one of the brothers bid him a teasing farewell: "Well, off you go, since you are so set on becoming a saint!"

"When you hear *me* called a saint," Ferdinand replied, "kneel down and thank God!"

When the new Franciscan—now called Anthony—arrived in Morocco in 1221, he became deathly ill. After only a few months, he was forced to return to Europe. He arrived in Italy just in time for the general meeting of the Friars Minor in Assisi. St. Francis himself was there, and Anthony felt honored to be in the founder's presence. His reticence hid his abilities from the superiors at the meeting, however, and they deployed him to the obscure hermitage of St. Paul near Forlì. He happily served there with the other brothers, mainly by working in the kitchen.

But Anthony's talents were discovered when Dominican and Franciscan friars attended an ordination at Forlì. Customarily, someone preached at such events, but on this occasion no one was prepared. So the group called on Anthony to speak whatever the Holy Spirit inspired. He begged to be let off, but the group insisted. Reluctantly, Anthony addressed the assembly. He began simply but soon overflowed with intricate reflections based on Scripture and the early Christian writers. Even though the brothers had eaten a hearty meal, no one dozed. They were astonished by the dishwasher's eloquence, passion, and wisdom. Informed of the friar whose real talents were buried at Forlì, the regional superior reassigned Anthony to preach throughout northern Italy.

Wherever Anthony went, crowds jammed churches to hear him preach. Often the buildings were too small to hold all those who gathered, so he spoke to thousands in city squares. Many of his hearers, including heretics who had come to watch the show, decided on the spot to reform their lives. Spiritual revival occurred wherever he spoke.

The Friars Minor couldn't help but notice Anthony's success. Though his brand of preaching was novel to them, they soon saw its value. St. Francis of Assisi's simple style of proclaiming the gospel, telling spontaneous stories, and offering his own dramatic example had produced a wave of renewal. Now the community's leaders recognized that Anthony's approach, combining oratory and learning with a charismatic gift, would generate a second one. The order wanted to train others to follow in his footsteps. In 1223, Francis himself appointed Anthony to teach theology to the friars. This was a first. Before this, Francis had been wary of study because he had feared scholarship might replace devotion in his brothers' hearts.

PRAYER AND HOLINESS
Adolphe Tanquerey (1854–1932)

The sanctifying power of prayer is such that the saints never tired of saying that he lives well who prays well. Prayer produces three marvelous effects: 1) it *detaches* us from creatures; 2) it *unites* us entirely to God; 3) it gradually *transforms* us into God.

Prayer detaches us from creatures in so far as they obstruct our union with God. This effect follows from prayer's very nature as an elevation of the heart to God. In order to be raised up to God we must first loosen the bonds that fasten us to creatures. . . .

Moreover, prayer makes our union with God more complete and more perfect day by day.

More *complete:* Prayer lays hold of all our faculties in order to unite them to God. It seizes the *higher faculties* of the soul: the mind, by absorbing it in the thought of divine things; the will, by directing it toward the glory of God and the welfare of souls; the heart, by permitting it to pour out its love into a Heart ever open, loving, ever merciful, and enabling it to produce affections that cannot be but sanctifying.

Prayer also seizes the *lower faculties* of the soul by helping us to fasten upon God and Our Lord, our imagination, our memory, our emotions, and even our passions in so far as they are capable of good.

Prayer even takes possession of our *body,* helping us to mortify our outward senses, which so often lead us astray, and to regulate our exterior according to the dictates of modesty.

More *perfect:* Prayer . . . produces in the soul acts of religion born of faith, sustained by hope and vivified by love. . . . Is there anything nobler, anything more sanctifying than these acts of the theological virtues? Prayer, likewise, presupposes the performance of acts of humility, of obedience, of fortitude, of constancy, so that it is not difficult to see that the holy exercise of prayer unites our soul to God in a most perfect manner.

No wonder, then, that through prayer the soul is gradually transformed into God. Prayer causes . . . a mutual exchange between us and God; while we offer him our homage and our requests, he stoops down to us and bestows on us his graces.

Of course, other friars could not reproduce the supernatural elements of St. Anthony's ministry unless God intervened. In fact, so many signs and wonders confirmed the saint's words that he is remembered as a miracle worker.

Perhaps Anthony's most famous miracle occurred when he preached to an audience of fish. As he addressed a rambunctious group of heretics who were heckling him, he became discouraged by their unwillingness to listen. He turned to the water nearby. "O fish," he said, "come and hear the word of God." Reportedly, he exhorted the fish to thankfulness for all God's gifts, among them "fins to swim where you will" and the privilege of being Christ's food before and after his resurrection. It is said that hundreds of fish gathered and listened attentively, heads above water, until he dismissed them with a blessing. Then some of the onlookers, touched by the miracle, rejected their errors and returned to the faith.

Once the whole city of Limoges shut down to hear him. Shops closed, and all business ceased. More than thirty thousand people assembled, too many even for the city square, and Anthony led them to an old Roman amphitheater. Just as he began to preach, the sky darkened, pregnant with a violent storm. People made a move to scatter, but he stopped them. "Friends, don't leave," he said. "Have confidence in God. I assure you in his name that he will not let one of you get wet." No one moved, and not a drop of rain fell in the theater. When the crowd filed out, however, they discovered that the surrounding area was flooded and covered with large hailstones.

Anthony also exercised gifts of prophecy and revelation. An official known for corruption once accosted him in the streets of Le Puy. Every day Anthony had politely bowed to the man, who thought the saint was mocking him. "If I did not fear God's anger," the official said, "I would spit you on my sword!"

"I once hoped for martyrdom," said Anthony, "but I was not worthy of it. But God has shown me that you will become a martyr. When that day comes, remember me and pray for me."

The official laughed in Anthony's face. Not long afterward, however, he had a change of heart. He sold his possessions, gave the money to the poor, and went on pilgrimage with his bishop to Jerusalem. There he vigorously argued issues of faith with a group of Saracens. They seized him, tortured him over three days, and on the fourth day led him out to be executed. On his way to his death, the man remembered Anthony's words and told bystanders that the saint had predicted his unlikely martyrdom.

In November 1225, Anthony preached in Brouges to a synod of two hundred bishops. All present were stunned when he railed at the archbishop, Simon de Sully, who was presiding. "You there, with the mitre, I'm talking to you!" he roared. He publicly reprimanded the archbishop for certain secret sins. Deeply moved, the prelate openly wept in repentance and afterward confided his weakness to Anthony. From that time, de Sully seemed to have experienced renewed zeal, vindicating himself with good behavior for the rest of his life.

Anthony customarily prayed late into the night. Several hosts, curious about their famous guest, spied on him at those times. They claim to have seen Anthony holding a beautiful child and conversing with him. Word got out that Christ came as a child and spoke with him, a scene that artists have fixed in the popular mind. In these depictions of St. Anthony and Christ, the child is often standing on an open book. Why do you suppose Christ would choose to come to Anthony not as an adult but as a little child? The place and time of the apparitions may offer a clue. Anthony was ministering in southern France, the home base of the Albigensians, who denied that Jesus was a human being and also opposed procreation because they believed all matter was evil. What better way for Christ to refute them than to appear as a child?

To this day, many people pray to St. Anthony to help them find something they have lost. Perhaps the custom has its roots in the following miracle. A Franciscan novice at the Montpellier house, where Anthony lived, decided to abandon the order. As he left the house, he took one of the saint's valuable manuscripts, a glossary on the psalms. The youth probably hoped to sell it to cover the cost of his escape. When Anthony missed the text, he prayed for its return. In a short time the novice, pale with fear, ran back into the house. Repentant, he returned the book and confessed his wrongdoing to Anthony. He claimed that a monstrous image had blocked his passage on a bridge and had threatened mayhem if he did not return the glossary. Anthony forgave the young man, who reconsidered his decision to leave and remained with the friars.

106 My favorite of all Anthony's wonders is a simple, loving gesture that occurred when he served as superior of the Dominican house at Limoges. Pierre, a novice, struggled with temptations to leave the community. One crisp evening Anthony encountered the young man walking on the monastery grounds. Driven by a profound sense of loneliness, Pierre was close to deciding that he could no longer stay with the friars. Anthony greeted the youth with only his eyes, seeming to look right into his anguished soul. Pierre certainly felt Anthony's love, and it must have seemed like a light in his darkness. Without asking any questions, Anthony gently placed his hands on the novice's shoulders and breathed into his mouth. "Receive the Holy Spirit, Pierre," he said. Immediately, the young man experienced a dramatic change of heart. Pierre lived to a ripe old age as a Franciscan and loved to repeat that story.

For the last five years of his life, Anthony lived in Padua. His ministry there stirred a great spiritual renewal and a general reform of conduct. He personally settled quarrels, arranged for the release of prisoners, and encouraged people to make restitution. He denounced the practice of usury and influenced the passage of laws that reformed the penalties for debtors. He died there in 1231.

"The ideal preacher," Anthony once wrote, "should be hard as flint. From him must spring the spark that gives light to the soul and enkindles in it the fire of divine love." That's a prescription for life-changing miracles. Anthony had described himself to a T.

The Freedom of Poverty

Poverty is an easy way to God.

Poverty is the mother of humility. It is as difficult to preserve humility amid riches as purity in the midst of delights and luxury.

Poverty sets free. When a person delights in and gloats over his possessions, in reality he limits, even loses his freedom. The mania of riches has enslaved him. He is lowered in status, being no longer the owner but the owned. He has subordinated himself to his goods.

Such servile subjection becomes evident in the fever that dominates him and the anguish that racks him when he loses some of his possessions. In short, true liberty is not found except in voluntary poverty.

Poverty is true riches. So precious is poverty that God's Only-Begotten Son came on earth in search of it. In heaven he had superabundance of all goods. Nothing was lacking there but poverty.

St. Anthony of Padua

107

The Miracle Is the Message
St. Vincent Ferrer (c. 1350–1419)

We must see Vincent Ferrer as having one foot in heaven.

HENRI GHÉON

St. Vincent Ferrer was a bona fide wonder-worker. Believe it or not, he performed his first miracle when he was still in the womb. A blind woman pressed her head against his mother's stomach and was instantly healed. Once asked how many miracles he had worked, Vincent modestly estimated 3,000. The church carefully documented 873 of these when it declared him a saint. You can't write long about Vincent Ferrer without mentioning wonders. His life was punctuated with them.

Even when Vincent Ferrer was a child, the people of Valencia, his hometown in Aragon, recognized his superior spiritual and intellectual gifts. In 1357, his parents dedicated their son to the service of the church. Eleven years later, Vincent became a member of the Friars Preachers, the religious order founded by St. Dominic. He was ordained a priest in 1378. At age twenty-eight, he had already earned fame as a theologian, teacher, preacher, and miracle worker.

Vincent's prodigies began to flow in full force in 1374 while he studied at Barcelona. Aragon's harvests failed that year, and as a result, famine and disease were rampant. Vincent advised the townspeople to beg God's mercy. One Sunday twenty thousand people marched to the city square, where Vincent called them to repentance. At the climax of his sermon, he prophesied that relief would come that day: "Have confidence, rejoice in God," he declared, "before night, two ships laden with grain will make port."

Few people believed him. Many raged with disbelief because the weather was so bad that it seemed unlikely any ships would reach the harbor. Vincent's forecast also annoyed his superior, who consequently forbade him to exercise his spiritual gifts without permission. That night, however, two supply ships arrived in Barcelona, and Vincent became an instant hero.

~~~

Vincent Ferrer worked his most famous miracle while he was under orders not to use his extraordinary powers. One day as he passed a construction site, a mason began to fall from the top of a building. "Brother Vincent," he cried out, "save me!"

"Stay where you are," shouted Vincent, "until I come back." According to eyewitnesses, the mason stopped, suspended in midair, while Vincent ran to get his superior's permission to perform a miracle.

"He's waiting?" asked the superior, stunned by Vincent's request.

"Yes," said Vincent.

"Well, go back and finish it off," said the superior. Vincent raced back to the hovering man.

"My superior says you may come down," said Vincent, and the man floated safely to the ground.

Such preternatural phenomena did not push Vincent's head into the clouds. Instead, he occupied himself with compassion for human beings. A friend to the rich and poor alike, he counseled those with grievous personal problems, taught penitents how to live good lives, and settled family quarrels. The preacher and prophet was also a man of public affairs, advising both princes and popes. If Vincent had one foot in heaven, he had planted the other firmly on earth.

109

~~~

The Great Western Schism had started the year Vincent was ordained. Rivals in Rome and Avignon claimed to be pope. For nearly forty years, the scandal rent Christendom, confusing the faithful throughout Europe. Vincent was loyal to Clement VII, the Avignon pope. He was also friend, confidant, and confessor to Clement's successor, Benedict XIII, who was elected in 1394.

Vincent consistently pressured Benedict XIII to cooperate with efforts to restore unity, but Benedict obstinately hindered every initiative. The tension of conflicting loyalties to friend and church finally eroded Vincent's health. Afflicted by the stress, he fell seriously ill in 1398.

While Vincent lay near death with fever, Jesus appeared to him. In the vision, the great preachers Dominic and Francis also came to comfort him. Jesus touched Vincent tenderly on the cheek, commanding him to get up. "You will go through the world, preaching," Jesus said, and at that Vincent arose, completely well. It is said that Jesus left permanent finger marks on his face.

Vincent took Jesus' words as a commission for the rest of his life. Armed with ecclesial authority to preach anywhere, he began his international mission in 1399. For the better part of twenty years, he journeyed four times through Spain, northern Italy, the Alpine countries, southern Germany, and France. He traveled on foot until an ulcerous leg forced him to ride a donkey.

Whenever Vincent approached a village, people brought out their sick so that he might cure them. Thousands of times he raised his handheld cross, and many people were healed. A dying baby would recover and laugh. An elderly cripple would toss his crutches aside and dance. A blind girl would brush against him and regain sight. He occasioned miraculous healings in every town, hundreds of times over.

Vincent preached nearly every day, and everywhere he went, thousands gathered to listen to him. Miracles enhanced his words, for even when he couldn't speak the language, everyone in the crowd heard him plainly in their own language, no matter how far they stood from him.

Vincent preached mainly about the folly of sin, the necessity of penance, and the imminence of the coming judgment. Like many saints before him, he believed that Jesus would come soon to wrap up human history. Referring to Revelation 14:6, he identified himself as the "angel of the judgment." Though he did not profess to be an angel in human form, he saw himself as Christ's messenger, bearing good news for the repentant and bad news for the hard-hearted.

Once while preaching in Salamanca, he demonstrated his claim with an extraordinary wonder. He commanded some grave diggers in the crowd to bring forward the body of a recently deceased woman.

"Dead woman," he reportedly shouted, "tell these people whether I am the Messenger of the Apocalypse sent to preach the coming of the Last Day."

The woman sat up and said, "Yes, Father, you are that messenger." Then she immediately fell back into her coffin, again a lifeless corpse.

All over Europe people responded to Vincent's preaching with tearful enthusiasm. Many reformed their lives. As many as three thousand people at a time followed him from town to town. Among these was a small group who performed public penance by scourging themselves. To prevent any accusations of evil, Vincent organized these penitents into a community that he closely governed. To his credit, in two decades no abuses marred his crusade.

⌒⌐

By 1414, three rivals claimed to be pope. That year a council of bishops at Constance deposed one pretender, asked the other two to resign, and arranged for a new election. Benedict XIII brushed off Vincent's appeal that he step down. Because Benedict stubbornly blocked unity that was vital to the church, Vincent urged his vast international following to withdraw their allegiance. With two claimants gone and Benedict isolated, a new pope was chosen and the schism was over. Vincent spent his last years in Brittany and Normandy and died in 1419.

⌒⌐

I confess that I did not like Vincent Ferrer much before I studied him. From what I knew, he seemed severe, arrogant, and—yes—a little weird. I soon discovered how mistaken I was. Vincent Ferrer was gentle, humble, and wise. As I watched him move with deft grace through the tormented fourteenth century, I began to admire and even to like him. His anguished times cried out for a saint like him. Vincent lived through the violence of the Hundred Years' War, the malevolence of the bubonic plague, and the turmoil of the Great Western Schism. The past century had its own share of turbulence—a hundred years of war, the new treacherous plague of AIDS, and shameful racial and religious divisions.

Where are our St. Vincent Ferrers? We desperately need them.

The Divine Light Within

You must open the interior eyes of your soul on the light, on this heaven within you, a vast horizon stretching far beyond the realm of human activity, an unexplored country to the majority of human beings. The ordinary observer sees in the ocean only the realm of storms and never guesses that a few feet below the surface its waters are always limpid, and in a scintillating clarity is found vegetation and living creatures of wondrous diversity, marvelous in beauty and structure, mysterious depths where the pearl is formed.

Such is the depth of the soul where God dwells and shows himself to us. And when the soul has seen God, what more can it want? If it possesses him, why and for whom can it ever be moved to abandon him?

So at any price, preserve yourself in that calm through which the soul sees the eternal Sun.

St. Vincent Ferrer

PART FIVE

MIRACLES *to* AWAKEN US

"Wake up, O sleeper,
   rise from the dead,
and Christ will shine on you."

Be very careful, then, how you live—not as unwise but as wise, making
the most of every opportunity, because the days are evil.

EPHESIANS 5:14–16

eresa of Ávila claimed that spiritually she was a late bloomer. Sometime after her fortieth birthday, she said, her soul experienced an awakening. We should take comfort in the assurance of this great saint's example— it's never too late. No matter how old or how set in our ways we may be, God still pursues us and wants to touch us with his love.

What's true for the individual Christian is true for all Christians. From earliest times the church itself has needed spiritual awakening. If you doubt it, just dip into St. Paul's letters. Try 1 Corinthians, where Paul felt obliged to correct evil practices that had crept into the community. Or try Galatians. Why do you suppose he addressed this New Testament church as "you foolish Galatians"?

That the church often needs to be shaken and aroused to spiritual realities should come as no surprise. God seems to have set it up that way. He created the church as a partnership between himself and human beings. Sometimes I wonder why God decided to tie himself to a bunch of sinners. "Didn't you realize," I want to ask him, "how badly we would mess things up?" Then I stop myself, realizing that he knew exactly what he was doing. He desired for the community of believers to have to rely entirely on him.

Look back to the sixteenth century. The church had descended to its nadir. Spiritual decadence had benumbed it, and political turmoil had wrenched it apart. Yet, in darkness that seemed too thick to dispel, bright lights of renewal began to shine. St. Francis of Paola stirred the Italian church to throbbing new life. His stupendous miracles were the talk of the whole peninsula. With singular wisdom and integrity, he brought people back to God on their knees.

A short time later, Teresa of Ávila spearheaded a spiritual awakening in Spain. She was a most practical mystic, a charming and savvy saint. Teresa was blessed with a diversity of gifts—contemplation, miracle working, political know-how, and pastoral care. She strategically employed them all to revivify faith throughout Spain.

In the nineteenth century, John Bosco's apostolate to rescue homeless boys sparked a renewal throughout northern Italy. Against odds that would stop most of us, he evangelized and cared for thousands of desperate young men. From these castoffs he recruited and formed a new religious order that would have a profound influence on the rest of the church. He did it all with nothing but faith in his arsenal. When he turned to God for aid, God didn't disappoint him. Every day of John Bosco's life was strewn with visions, revelations, signs, and miracles.

And what about Francis of Assisi? He launched a movement that brought spiritual reformation to all of thirteenth-century Europe. His tiny, ragtag band of followers miraculously multiplied into thousands in a few short years. Almost eight hundred years later, the church still draws refreshment from his radical decision to follow Christ.

Two compelling facts stand out from the example of these four saints. First, spiritual awakening emerges neither from clever programs nor detailed strategies; it comes one heart at a time. Second, God sometimes chooses to bring spiritual replenishment to millions through one person's life of faith.

None of these saints set out to found religious communities. None had planned to spawn renewals or to reform the church. Their aims were more personal. They simply wanted to love God above anything else—a goal we would be wise to make our own.

116

Miracles for the Poor

St. Francis of Assisi (1181–1226)

You will never understand Francis till you realize that with all the love and loyalty of his heart he married Poverty for Christ's sake. She was the Princess Poverty.

C. C. MARTINDALE, S. J.

The people of Assisi thought Francis was crazy.

Francis gave them plenty of evidence for their view. What would *you* say about a rich kid who seemed to change overnight from party-goer to ascetic? who swapped his fine clothes for a beggar's rags, gleefully renounced his inheritance, and stripped naked in a bishop's court? who kissed lepers, preached to birds, and claimed that Jesus spoke to him from a crucifix?

Had I personally observed Francis's unusual behavior, I think I might have agreed with his critics. "Of course I favor taking Christianity seriously," I might have said, "but Francis has gone too far." No doubt I would have echoed the voice of reason, warning of extremism and praising balance.

Francis certainly was an extremist. But weren't all the saints? While it's true that he was unbalanced, in the sense that he did not limit his enthusiasm, Francis was anything but insane. To the contrary, you could argue that he had a healthier mind than most of us. Unlike him, we focus narrowly on the material world. We wear blinders that shut out the broader and deeper spiritual realm. By so doing, we place ourselves out of touch with a vast part of reality. So perhaps we are the ones who are a little crazy.

Francis's view was spiritually panoramic. When he observed the ordinary, he perceived it with a breadth and depth we often miss. He looked beyond the human to behold the divine.

Born in Assisi in 1181, Francis was the son of Peter Bernardone, a successful merchant who thought the world of his son. As a youth,

Francis was infatuated with the romantic world of chivalry and sometimes imagined himself as an armored knight. He dreamed of fame and glory and was not much interested in formal education or his father's business. As a wealthy youth, he preferred to organize parties for the town's young people. Though never a profligate, he enjoyed his role as leader of the revelers. Even so, he gave generously to the poor.

Francis's conversion occurred more gradually than most people imagine. During a civil war in 1201, he was captured and imprisoned in Perugia. After a year he was released, only to be afflicted with a serious illness. Characteristically, he bore both his imprisonment and the disease with cheerful patience, though afterward he was more serene and serious.

On his recovery, he decided to fight in a war that was raging in southern Italy. In hopes of joining the army of Duke Walter III of Brienne, he outfitted himself lavishly. One day, however, he met a poor man in shabby clothes. Overcome by compassion, the would-be warrior traded his expensive suit of armor for the beggar's rags.

That same night, Francis had a prophetic dream, which at first he misunderstood. He envisioned a great castle packed with armaments bearing the sign of the cross. He thought he heard a voice say that the weapons were for him and his soldiers. He also sensed that a lovely bride awaited him there. This was all true enough, but Francis did not yet understand that these would be spiritual warriors and his spiritual bride.

Encouraged by this vision, Francis set out to join the duke's army. He never arrived. He took ill again en route. On his sickbed he heard a divine voice ask, "Which is better? To serve the servant or the Lord?"

"Of course, to serve the Lord," Francis answered.

"Then why make a master of the servant?" said the voice.

Francis began to get the idea. When he returned to Assisi, he resumed his former pattern of life, but he had lost his enthusiasm for it. His friends noticed that he seemed distracted amid the merriment and suggested that perhaps he had fallen in love. "Yes," said Francis, "I am going to take a wife more beautiful and more worthy than any you know." In the squalor of Assisi's back streets, Francis had caught sight of Lady Poverty. She had captivated him, and he was determined to embrace her.

Francis took some hesitant steps toward her by devoting himself to prayer. He also made a pilgrimage to Rome, where he spent a day as a beggar. The experience revolted him. He returned home still nauseated by the stench of the city's back streets and repulsed by the humiliation that he saw there. He started to give alms publicly, right from his own door. However, these charitable acts made him feel condescending and paternalistic. Instead of looking down on the poor, he wanted to look up to them.

One day, while riding on the Assisi plain, Francis gave alms to a leper. It was a decisive step. As Francis offered his gift, he suppressed his disgust and kissed the leper's hand. In turn, the leper lifted his face and gave Francis the kiss of peace. At that, something broke deep inside of Francis.

A miracle expedited Francis's conversion and set the course of his life. One day he was praying in the church of St. Damian, on the outskirts of Assisi. Suddenly a voice from a crucifix said to him three times, "Francis, go and repair my house, which you see is falling down." Francis shook with terror, and at that moment he was profoundly changed. Thomas of Celano, Francis's first biographer, saw in this event the source of the saint's unwavering devotion to the crucified Christ.

Francis thought that God had told him to repair the church of St. Damian, which was literally collapsing. In a misguided moment, he sold some of his father's merchandise and offered the money to the priest at St. Damian. Terrified of Francis's belligerent father, the priest prudently declined the gift, so Francis left it on a windowsill.

When he discovered what Francis had done, Peter Bernardone was hurt and enraged. He beat his son mercilessly and locked him up in chains. He dragged Francis before Bishop Guido of Assisi to have him settle the issue. Then Bernardone issued an ultimatum. Francis could pay for the goods he had taken and return home, or else he could forfeit his inheritance. At the bishop's direction, Francis agreed to pay for the merchandise. Then he renounced his inheritance with a dramatic gesture. "The clothes I wear are also his," Francis declared. "I will give them back." With that, he stripped off all of his clothes. Then he turned to his father. "Up till now I have called you father on earth," he said. "From now on I say, 'Our Father, who art in heaven.'"

For several years Francis roamed the roads of central Italy, shabbily dressed and carrying a pilgrim's staff. He returned to Assisi to beg money to complete the reconstruction of St. Damian's. Similarly, he arranged for the repair of St. Mary of the Angels, nicknamed the Portiuncula, or "little piece."

At this church in 1209, a spiritual insight revealed to Francis the life pattern that he and his disciples would follow. One day at Mass, a particular Scripture passage, Matthew 10:7–10, struck him profoundly: "As you go, preach this message: 'The kingdom of heaven is near.' Heal the sick, raise the dead, cleanse those who have leprosy, drive out demons. Freely you have received, freely give. Do not take along any gold or silver or copper in your belts; take no bag for the journey, or extra tunic, or sandals or a staff." Francis took these words as God's personal direction to him.

Francis embraced this gospel ideal with no hesitation. He shed his extra clothes and his shoes, keeping only a coat that he tied about himself with a cord. He went from town to town, urging everyone to repent. Everywhere, his words and example moved people deeply. He charmed his hearers by presenting the demands of the gospel in the romantic language of the troubadours. He would later implement the commands to heal people and set them free.

During these years Francis accumulated a band of followers. By 1210, a dozen men had embraced his ideals. They wore habits of undyed woolen coats tied with cords, the dress of poor peasants. Francis offered them a simple life consisting of the requirements of the gospel. He called his brothers the Friars Minor. They were to be "lesser" because he wanted them to take the low position of servants. That year, Francis went to Rome to seek approval for his community from Pope Innocent III. Prompted by a vision of Francis holding up a falling church building, the pope gave verbal consent and commissioned the Friars Minor to preach repentance.

During Francis's rebuilding of St. Damian's, he had often prophesied that someday it would be a convent. "Help me finish this building," he said. "Here one day will be a monastery of nuns who will bring glory to the Lord throughout the church." Now, years later in 1212, Clare of Assisi joined Francis, starting a community of women committed to his life pattern. Francis's prophecy about St. Damian's came true when she and her sisters took up residence there.

<hr />

Preaching Christ crucified and loving him in the poor dominated Francis's attention. It was the heart of his ministry. Miracles, visions, and prophecies occurred plentifully, but they were only side effects. He barely noticed them. Here is just a sampler:

Once, in Spoleto, a man with a cancerous face met Francis. Hideously malformed, the man tried to throw himself at Francis's feet. Francis, however, stopped him. He took the man's diseased face in his hands and kissed him on both cheeks. Immediately, the man was healed of all disfigurement. "I don't know which I ought to wonder at most," said St. Bonaventure, a later follower of St. Francis, "such a kiss or such a cure."

When Francis visited Toscanella, he boarded at a soldier's home. The man's small son was crippled and confined to a cradle. Completely immobile, the little boy had never even crawled. At first, Francis refused the soldier's requests to heal his child, because Francis felt he was unworthy to ask for such a great grace. But finally he prayed, laid his hand on the boy, and made the sign of the cross over him. Then Francis lifted the child from his crib and set him on his feet. Healed, the lad showed his new strength by walking—probably strutting quite proudly—all about the house.

One day in Gubbio, a woman with severely deformed hands ran up to Francis. "Just touch them," she pleaded as she raised her misshapen hands to him. Francis clasped her hands in his, gently moved his fingers over hers, and she was healed. What do you think she did next? What any Italian woman would do. She used her restored hands to cook. She went off and baked a cheesecake for Francis. He ate some of it and sent the rest back to her family.

Everyone knows that wild creatures of every sort miraculously became tame in Francis's presence. Thomas of Celano tells of the rabbit and the pheasant who could not bear to be separated from him; of the friendly falcon who awakened Francis at night for prayer but did not do so when the saint was sick; of the cricket who would rest in Francis's hand and sing at his request; and of many others. Thus, Francis is honored as the patron saint of animal lovers.

Francis especially liked birds, and a popular account tells how he once preached to them. However, Francis liked birds in more ways than one, as the following story shows. Once, while traveling through Spain, Francis became sick. While recovering, he confessed to his companion that he would very much like to eat a bird, if he had one. At that, a man on horseback rode up and gave Francis a fine fowl, already prepared for cooking. Francis received the gift with relish and soon enjoyed his impromptu barbecue. I particularly like this anecdote because it removes the romantic veneer from St. Francis by showing his humanity, a side of him we rarely see.

Once, in the early days, Francis prophesied to a few friars that a great number of men would join them. He also foretold that the Friars Minor would spread throughout the world. By the general meeting of the order in 1221, his words had come true. The friars had established centers in Italy, Spain, France, Germany, and Hungary. In time, he regretted that his community had grown so large. Many new members of the order favored owning property and thus threatened Francis's commitment to Lady Poverty. However, in 1223, Pope Honorius III officially approved a rule for the Friars Minor that embodied Francis's ideals. Still, controversy over worldly concerns such as possessions seethed in the order and eventually divided it.

In 1224, Francis retired with only one companion to a tiny hermitage on Mount Alvernia. Here an extraordinary miracle occurred. One day Francis had a vision of a great seraph, a high-ranking angel, who was nailed to a cross. As Francis beheld this apparition, nail marks appeared on his own hands and feet. A gaping wound opened on his right side, as if he had been pierced with a lance. This painful, physical replication of Christ's wounds is called the stigmata, a phenomenon reserved for only a few mystics. How are we to understand this mysterious and mystical experience? One way is to view the stigmata as a marvelous sign of Francis's extraordinary intimacy with the crucified Christ.

Francis died in 1226. People had ceased thinking he was crazy long before. Rather, as with Mother Teresa in our day, they had welcomed him everywhere as a living saint. In a dozen years, St. Francis had initiated a movement that would bring new life to the church throughout thirteenth-century Europe. His ability to enchant souls continues. Over the centuries, he has awakened hundreds of thousands of his followers to the light of the Spirit.

123

Prayer to Christ Crucified

We adore you, Christ, here and in all your churches which are in the whole world, and we bless you because by your holy cross you have redeemed the world.

St. Francis of Assisi

A Miracle in Her Soul

ST. TERESA OF ÁVILA (1515–82)

Come, Creator, Spirit, come
From your bright heavenly throne,
Come, take possession of our souls
And make them all your own. . . .

O guide our minds with your blest light
With love our hearts inflame. . . .

"VENI CREATOR SPIRITUS"

Some devoted students of the saints exalt them too highly. These overzealous hagiographers do the saints a great disservice. They daub their subjects' blemishes with cosmetic religiosity. They seal saints in airtight wrappers or isolate them on pedestals. Haven't you read biographies of saints who are made to seem like visitors from other planets? Such well-intentioned writers also do us a great disservice. They put the saints beyond our reach by concealing their humanity.

I find these spiritual giants more attractive when their mortality plainly shows. When, among their wonders, I see their wrongdoings and weaknesses, I can relate to them more easily.

It is unlikely that any hagiographer, no matter how uncritical or pious, could obscure the humanness of Teresa of Ávila. If a biographer attempted to put Teresa on a pedestal, I'm convinced she would hastily climb down. "I didn't like it up there very much," she would say. "From silly devotions and sour-faced saints," she once said, "good Lord deliver us!"

Teresa herself was anything but silly or sour-faced. This splendid woman was graced with heavenly ecstasies but never ceased to enjoy earthly creatures. "I could be bribed with a sardine," she once confessed. Teresa bore her radiance in a clay pot. Her life seemed to be a perfect blend of the natural and the supernatural, the human and the divine. Once, a visitor was shocked to find the holy woman delightfully devouring a partridge someone had given her. Was this the way of the ascetic? What would people think? "Let them think what they please," said Teresa, licking her fingers. "There's a time for partridge and a time for penance." Is it any wonder that Teresa has such universal appeal?

We love Teresa of Ávila for her candid self-revelation. She does not tell us about her raptures without also confessing her faults. We admire her intelligent approach to spirituality. Teresa invites us to discipline ourselves in prayer and, in the same breath, casually reminds us to relax and recreate. We appreciate her view that common sense is a prerequisite to the spiritual life. Innocent of sentimentality, she refreshes us. "Even though the Lord should give this young girl devotion," she once wrote, "and teach her contemplation, if she has no sense she never will come to have any, and instead of being of use to the community she will be a burden." Here's one of Teresa's delicious exclamations that failed to make it into any of my saint books. "May God preserve us from stupid nuns!" Oh, to have been able to quote that line when I was in fourth grade!

PRAY FOR DIVINE LIGHT
Bl. Angela of Foligno (c. 1248–1309)

No one can be saved without divine light. Divine light causes us to begin and to make progress, and it leads us to the summit of perfection. Therefore if you want to begin and to receive this divine light, pray. If you have begun to make progress, pray. And if you have reached the summit of perfection, and want to be super-illumined so as to remain in that state, pray.

If you want faith, pray. If you want hope, pray. If you want charity, pray. If you want poverty, pray. If you want obedience, pray. If you want chastity, pray. If you want humility, pray. If you want meekness, pray. If you want fortitude, pray. If you want any virtue, pray.

And pray in this fashion: always reading the Book of Life, that is, the life of the God-man, Jesus Christ, whose life consisted of poverty, pain, contempt and true obedience.

In 1535, at age twenty, Teresa entered the Carmelite convent of the Incarnation at Ávila. By her own admission, over the next twenty years her progress in the spiritual life was spotty and slow. Life was lax at the monastery, where the sisters indulged in a somewhat worldly, freewheeling social life. Teresa was no exception. She later described herself as quite a "gadabout." But things changed when she turned forty. Inspired moments with Augustine's Confessions and a picture of the suffering Christ persuaded Teresa to renew her commitment to serious prayer. At that time she began to receive visions and interior communications from God.

Such spiritual phenomena were controversial in sixteenth-century Spain, as they still are. To determine their genuineness, a spiritual adviser directed Teresa to seek only those things most pleasing to God. He told her to pray daily the "Veni Creator Spiritus," the ancient invocation of the Holy Spirit.

One day as Teresa prayed that lovely hymn, she was caught up for the first time in ecstasy. She heard within her these words: "I will not have you hold conversations with men, but with angels." Thereafter, the trickle of Teresa's mystical experiences swelled to a torrent. One of her visions was a terrifying revelation of the horrors of hell that galvanized her faith and commitment.

Teresa tried her best to keep her divine communications secret, but Ávila was a small town, and word got out. For several years, she suffered greatly from accusations of hypocrisy and demonism. Finally, however, St. Peter of Alcántara, a widely respected spiritual director, declared that she was clearly being led by the Spirit.

The great miracle in Teresa's life was not something she did but something that was done to her. As she grew in intimacy with God, she repeatedly experienced an extraordinary palpable sign of his closeness. It was as though God literally took possession of her heart and set it aflame with love.

Following is her own description of the divine invasion of her soul: "I saw an angel close by me, on my left side, in bodily form. He was not large, but small of stature and most beautiful—his face burning, as if he were one of the highest angels, who seem to be all of fire. . . . I saw in his hand a long spear of gold, and at the iron's point there seemed to be a little flame. He appeared to me to be thrusting it at times into my heart, and to pierce my very entrails; when he drew it out, he seemed to draw them out also, and to leave me all on fire with a great love of God."

The popular mind identifies this vision with Teresa. Artists and sculptors have often depicted it, the most famous representation being the seventeenth-century statue by Giovanni Bernini. St. John of the Cross, Teresa's friend and contemporary, described Teresa's experience as "the cauterization of her soul." He saw it as a profound mystical event reserved for a very few.

Words cannot describe what really happened to her. Teresa says that God touched her heart in a delightful yet painful way, leaving her soul afire with love for him. An astonishing fact witnessed to the truth of her words: According to a physician's testimony, after her death, St. Teresa's heart was found to bear a long, deep scar.

Perhaps the best expression of Teresa's mysticism is her activism. Her heaven-sent ecstasies seemed to focus her attention on earthly concerns. She demonstrated her love for God through her service to others. Only two years old when Martin Luther launched the Protestant movement, she later became a Catholic reformer during the Age of Reformation. By the time she was an adult, the Reformation was in full swing throughout Europe. Teresa contributed to the Catholic Reformation by awakening the religious ardor of men and women everywhere. Throughout Spain, she established renewed communities that adhered closely to the original Carmelite rule of life.

⌒

One September evening in 1560, Teresa and a few friends discussed the unhappy state of affairs at the convent of the Incarnation. They decried the lax observance of the rule, the predominance of cliques, and the excessive involvement with the outside world. Teresa probably expressed her strongly held opinion that too many sisters were jammed together into one place. "Experience has taught me," she said, "what a house full of women is like. God preserve us from such a state." During the conversation, Maria de Campo, Teresa's niece, made a lighthearted suggestion. "We'd probably be better off to start over at a new convent," she said. "Maybe then we could become real followers of the hermits of Mount Carmel."

For Teresa the idea was no joke. Believing that the Holy Spirit had inspired her niece's suggestion, she soon had things underway. Before long, she had secured financial backing and permission from the Carmelites and the church. But opposition erupted immediately. First, the people of Ávila cried out against the idea. The town, they said, could not possibly afford to support another monastery. Then the sisters at the convent of the Incarnation raised their voices in protest. Teresa's plan cut too close to the bone, threatening their comfortable lifestyle. And one day, a priest railed from the pulpit against wandering nuns who tried to start new religious orders. A few heads turned to gape at Teresa, who sat toward the back of church, chuckling quietly. She was laughing because she expected God to act, and he did.

Visions assured Teresa that God wanted her to establish the new community. Behind the scenes, her friends worked to garner official support. Money arrived miraculously just when it was needed. Teresa secretly constructed a small house as her future convent, pretending that the building was a home for the family of her married sister, Juana.

An accident on the construction site occasioned a charming miracle. Juana's little son, Gonzalez, was playing with pieces of stone when a wall collapsed, crushing him. Juana howled with anguish when she dug his broken body out of the rubble, because to all appearances, her child was dead. His father rushed the lifeless boy to Teresa, who took him in her arms, lowered her veil, and bent her head close to his. She breathed a prayer over her nephew. Instantly, Gonzalez revived, as if waking from sleep, and began to play with Teresa's face, his little fingers tracing a smile on her lips. God's touch had healed the child. Later, Gonzalez often teased his aunt about this incident. "Aunt Teresa," he would say, "you'd better be praying hard for me. It's your fault that I'm not already with God in heaven."

Amid much commotion, Teresa and four sisters opened the convent of St. Joseph on August 24, 1562. Gradually, opposition died down, and the sisters won the respect of all. Within five years, the Carmelites and the church were encouraging Teresa to establish additional monasteries. King Philip II encouraged the Catholic Reformation and strongly supported the renewal of convents and monasteries. Between 1567 and 1582, Teresa founded seventeen reformed Carmelite convents throughout Spain.

For her sisters, Teresa prescribed a simple life, rigorously based on the primitive Carmelite rule. Given her convictions about size, she allowed only thirteen women in a convent. The sisters lived in poverty, supporting themselves by begging. They spent long periods in silence and solitude and wore uncomfortable habits made from coarse serge. They went without shoes, wearing only sandals, and thus the new community got its name—the Discalced Carmelites. But Teresa also punctuated the seriousness of convent life with fun. With tambourines, dances, and improvised songs, the sisters frequently celebrated Christian feasts and special occasions. None of her sisters had a chance to become "sour faced."

Two little miracles that occurred in the early days at St. Joseph's characterize Teresa's wit and work. One involved a plague of lice. The other, a well.

First, her wit. One day the sisters determined to get rid of hordes of lice that had infested their rough clothing. Early in the morning the nuns marched in processions all through the house to the chapel, carrying crosses and singing psalms. They implored God to free them from the parasites. Then Teresa made the sign of the cross over her sisters, their rooms, and their beds, singing a spontaneous song with this delightful refrain, "Do Thou keep all nasty creatures out of this serge!" Immediately the lice vanished and never plagued the sisters again.

Second, her life's work. St. Joseph's Convent lacked a water supply. In fact, the water on the property was inaccessibly deep and rumored to be undrinkable. Against expert advice, Teresa sank a well, from which fresh, clear water flowed. Today, more than four hundred years later, Teresa's well still provides water for the convent!

When Teresa was a child, a picture of Jesus speaking with the Samaritan woman at the well hung on a wall in her room. She often stood before it and prayed, "Lord, give me of that water that I may not thirst." Now, quite appropriately, the well at St. Joseph's is called Samaritan's Well.

Prayer Cultivates Virtue

The beginner must think of himself as setting out to make a garden in which the Lord is to take his delight, yet in soil most unfruitful and full of weeds. His Majesty uproots the weeds and will set good plants in their stead. We have now, by God's help like good gardeners, to make these plants grow. We must water them carefully, so that they may not perish, but may produce flowers which shall send forth great fragrance to give refreshment to this Lord of ours, so that he may often come into the garden to take his pleasure and his delight among these virtues.

St. Teresa of Ávila

Raising the Dead and Other Miracles

St. Francis of Paola (1416–1507)

Heal the sick, raise the dead, cleanse those who have leprosy, drive out demons. Freely you have received, freely give. Do not take along any gold or silver or copper in your belts.

Matthew 10:8–9

St. Francis of Paola worked a wide variety of miracles, more diverse than those of any other mystic we've looked at. He seems to have possessed a comprehensive authority over nature akin to that of Christ himself. When Francis gave a command "in the name of charity," earth, fire, water, disease, and death all obeyed. For example, he defied gravity to move huge boulders. He passed through fire and handled glowing coals unharmed. He redirected streams with a word. He healed the blind. He raised the dead. Repeatedly.

Francis was so simple and his miracles so extraordinary that it's easy to miss the significance of his life and work. Focusing on the wonders might give the false impression that he was a show-off or a weirdo. Thus, a little background will help us appreciate him properly.

131

Francis of Paola founded a community of priests and brothers that he called the Minims, which means the "least." He and his followers imitated the humility and poverty of Francis of Assisi, his namesake. In 1435, Francis started his first monastery in Paola, his hometown in Calabria, located in the heel of the Italian boot. Francis was not formally educated and was never ordained a priest, but he was a gifted evangelist and pastor. His charismatic personality attracted hundreds of followers, whom he formed in the spiritual disciplines and built into strong brotherhoods. Before his death, Francis established Minim communities in Italy, Sicily, and France.

When Francis came on the scene, grave dangers were menacing both church and state. At the turn of the sixteenth century, internecine wars racked Italy. The city-states were in conflict with the popes, who at the time headed a secular state as well as the church. Worse yet, the Turks, who had overrun the eastern part of Europe and the Mediterranean Sea, were threatening to conquer the western countries. At the same time, serious problems plagued the church. Piety was at a low ebb, devotion was distorted, and corruption and neglect were on the rise in the ecclesiastical bureaucracies.

Amid these darkening circumstances, Francis of Paola shone as a beacon of integrity and holiness. He and his brothers spawned spiritual renewal everywhere they were located, especially in southern Italy. Francis's dynamic gifts and practical wisdom caught the attention of state and church alike. During his lifetime, he counseled and confronted five kings and seven popes.

Francis worked many of his earliest miracles during the construction of his first monastery in 1435. One day, a huge boulder sat in the middle of the site. Try as they might, the workmen could not dislodge it. So Francis knelt in prayer, and the gigantic stone popped out of the ground. A flabbergasted construction crew easily rolled it aside. On another day an immense rock began to rumble down a hill toward the workers. "In the name of charity, stop!" shouted Francis, and it stopped dead. He also stretched a beam that was too short, lifted an enormous log the workmen couldn't budge, and provided drinking water by striking the ground with a stick—always "in the name of charity," because Francis thought only of loving others.

Twice he revived fatally injured workers. He once knelt in prayer beside the body of a man crushed by a beam. Francis touched the mangled corpse with some herbs, and the workman got up, as though he had been simply taking a nap. A falling tree killed another laborer named Domenico Sapio. "In the name of charity, Domenico, arise!" commanded Francis. Domenico got up, brushed himself off, thanked Francis, and returned to work as if nothing had happened.

Francis's fame as a wonder-worker quickly spread throughout Calabria. Rich and poor came to him seeking miraculous help. Giacomo di Tarsia, a local baron, came to the monastery with his wife, Giovanna, and a retinue of friends and servants. He asked Francis to heal an abscess that doctors had said might require amputation of his leg. Francis sent one of the monks to his vegetable garden to pick some blades of an herb called "horse's toenail." Then Francis went alone to the chapel to pray. When he returned, he placed three blades of the herb over the baron's sore, bandaged it, and told him to go home. A few miles down the road from Paola, Giacomo said to his wife, "Giovanna, my leg does not hurt anymore." When the baron removed the wrap, he discovered that the abscess was completely gone. With whoops of laughter, he dismounted from his horse and ran about to show off his healing.

Francis cured the deaf, the mute, and the blind. From birth, Bartolo di Scigliano could neither hear nor speak. The doctors could do nothing for the little boy, and as a last resort his parents brought him to Francis. He sat down and stood Bartolo on his knee so that the boy and he would be face-to-face. Francis prayed briefly, then said with a smile, "My son, repeat after me, 'Jesus, Jesus, Jesus.'" During an agonizing moment of silence, the parents feared that nothing had happened. Then, "Jesus!" stammered the boy. The parents gasped with awe as, louder and more clearly, their son spoke. "Jesus!" Finally, shaking with excitement, little Bartolo shouted, "Jesus!" God's touch had changed his life forever.

Seventeen-year-old Giulia Catalano was born sightless. Her parents brought her to Francis, who was working in the garden. He greeted the family and then turned to Giulia. "Would you like me to ask God to give you your sight?" he asked.

"Oh, yes, Brother Francis, please pray for me," she replied.

Francis blessed an herb he held in his hands and touched it to Giulia's eyes. All watched expectantly. When he removed his fingers from the girl's face, she could see. Giulia blinked and—wide-eyed—

looked right at Francis. Her first experience with sight was to look upon the face of the wonder-worker who had healed her.

A young couple's infant son was born without eyes and with a deformed face. Crazed with anger and despair, the parents had nearly given up hope when they heard of the miracle worker in Calabria. The distraught father took his baby to Francis, wondering if he could do something for the child. "God loves your son," Francis said. "Don't be afraid. I will pray and ask him to heal the baby." Then he knelt in prayer and raised his arms to heaven. He wet his index finger with saliva and traced eyes on the infant's misshapen face. "In the name of charity," he said, "little brother, open your eyes!" Instantly the baby's eyes appeared, and he looked around in wonder. Dazzled with joy, the boy's father choked up and began to weep. Francis continued to touch the infant's face until normal features replaced all disfigurements. When he was satisfied that the boy's healing was complete, he placed him in his father's arms. A smiling father returned home, bearing a smiling baby.

134

Word of the Calabrian wonder-worker spread throughout Europe. Pope Paul II, who sought ways to bring spiritual renewal to the church, took an interest in Francis. In 1470, he sent his trusted associate, Fr. Girolamo Adorno, to investigate Francis's activities. The pope wanted to know more about his miracles, his severe pattern of life, and his growing number of followers and monasteries.

Adorno greeted Francis in church and tried to kiss his hand. The saint politely refused the gesture and startled the papal envoy with a fact he could only have known by revelation. "I should be kissing your hand," said Francis, "which has been consecrated for priestly service for more than thirty years." Later that day, Adorno attempted to persuade Francis to mitigate the severity of his community's pattern of life. The Minims disciplined themselves rigorously, observing a strict lifelong fast and abstaining from meat and dairy products. "You can withstand these rigors because you are a sturdy peasant," said Adorno. "But it isn't wise to impose such austerity on others who might not be able to survive it."

Francis silently walked over to a charcoal fire. With his bare hands he scooped up burning coals and, unharmed, held them before the stunned priest. "Yes, Father," he said, "I am only an unlearned peasant, and if I were not, I would not be able to do this." Adorno did not miss the subtlety of this dramatic reply.

Before the priest returned to Rome, he interviewed many of the people who had been miraculously cured. Among them were Baron Giacomo di Tarsia, whose leg abscess Francis had cured, and Francesco Rocco, the disfigured infant he had healed, who was now a handsome young man.

Impressed by the results of his inquiry, Fr. Adorno returned to assure the pope of Francis's authenticity. Paul II was pleased but still withheld approval of the Minims because he felt the strict fast endangered the well-being of the monks. But his successor, Pope Sixtus IV, after further investigations, gave blanket approval to the order in 1473.

The mounting Turkish threat to southern Italy alarmed Francis. He spoke urgently of the impending danger, exhorting everyone to prayer and repentance. He prophesied that Otranto, a port at the tip of the peninsula, would fall to the Turks on July 28, 1480. Francis wrote two letters to Ferdinand, king of Naples. He urged the king to quit meddling in Italian quarrels and to protect his eastern cities from the Turks. The king ignored Francis, whom he regarded as a religious fanatic. Otranto fell to the Turks on the exact day Francis had designated. That caught the king's attention. He redirected his armies, but it took fourteen months to win the city back.

Francis continued to warn Ferdinand to stop oppressing his people. He publicly admonished the king to establish a humane administration. Annoyed by Francis's constant opposition and the opening of new monasteries in Naples, Ferdinand ordered his arrest. The soldiers sent to capture Francis searched the monastery but could not find him. A workman challenged the captain of the troops. "How can it be," he asked, "that you do not see the servant of God? You have passed him many times."

"Where is he then?" demanded the angry captain. The worker led him to the church, where Francis was praying in the sanctuary. He had been invisible to the soldiers, who had searched the church several times.

The captain fell to his knees when he finally saw Francis. "In the name of charity, get up!" said Francis. "Tell the king for me that he is a man of little faith if he believes that my presence would help him. Tell him he had better change his behavior and reform his government or else he and his household will not avoid God's judgment."

Impressed by Francis's miraculous powers and strength of character, the captain persuaded Ferdinand to stop harassing him. But Ferdinand did not change his ways, and the saint's prophetic warning came true. Two decades later, the Spanish conquered Naples and overthrew Ferdinand's descendants.

136

In 1481, King Louis XI of France was slowly dying in the aftermath of a serious stroke. He asked Francis to come and heal him. At first Francis refused. However, the king appealed to Pope Sixtus IV, and the pope told Francis to go. When he arrived, Louis fell on his knees and begged for healing.

"The lives of kings," said Francis, "are in the hands of God and have divinely appointed limits. You should address your prayers to him."

Francis had received a revelation that the king would not survive the illness. The king persisted in his requests, but without success. Over time Francis's kindness won his confidence, and the two became friends. By Francis's word and example, Louis seems to have reckoned with God. Peacefully accepting his fate, he began to consult Francis regularly on personal and political matters. When the king died, he was resting in the saint's arms.

Francis never returned to Calabria. He remained twenty-five years in the French court, where he became a trusted adviser to the kings of France and a representative of the pope.

In his youth, Francis of Paola once revived his pet lamb, Martinello, after the animal was killed by some local workmen. That was just practice, I suppose. As Francis matured, he became much more than a wonder-worker. I like to think of him as a Christian statesman with marvelous powers, an ambassador for the gospel who performed miracles as he went about his work.

Farewell Letter

Sons of mine, whom I so love in the charity of Jesus Christ, I am separating myself from you to go to France. Hear the recommendations that I as your father in Jesus Christ leave with you. Love above all else our merciful Father in heaven, and serve him with all your strength and purity of heart.

Maintain and mortify your members with a salutary and discreet penance, which will not permit you to fall victim to the insidious lures of the devil. He cannot triumph except over those who are slothful and negligent. In the trials and temptations we face regularly in our daily lives, help one another.

Obey with humility your superiors, for obedience is the backbone of faith. Be sympathetic to the weaknesses and failings of others. Persevere in your holy vocation, to which the Lord has so obviously called you. Keep in mind that the crown of salvation is won only by those who persevere. It is vain to begin a good action unless you bring it to full completion. Maintain yourselves with holy emulation on the path of virtue, which I have so ardently pursued, particularly the practice of charity, humility, and patience.

Good-bye, my priests and brothers. We shall never again see each other on earth! May the Lord unite us in heaven!

St. Francis of Paola to his brothers, February 1483

An Astonishing Invasion of the Supernatural

St. John Bosco (1815–88)

In his life the supernatural almost became the natural, the extraordinary, the ordinary.

POPE PIUS XI

I think God may have smiled at the joke he played when he sent St. John Bosco as a gift to nineteenth-century Europe. He was a wonder-worker among people who did not believe in miracles.

Revolution ruled nineteenth-century Europe. Rebels toppled kings and kingdoms. War and conquest forged new nations. Patriots built democracies. Darwin and Marx spun new ideas that would radically alter the human experience. Emphasis was on the material, the natural, the power of humankind to set its own directions. The movers and shakers of culture denigrated the supernatural, the church, and even God.

St. John Bosco appeared as a sign of contradiction in this age of unbelief. During his lifework of caring for homeless boys, he performed thousands of miracles. They seemed to slip out of him. Hardly a day passed without his precipitating some supernatural intervention—a revelation, a prophecy, a mysterious appearance, a multiplication of food, a healing. So numerous and extraordinary were John Bosco's miracles that one of his biographers described his life as "an astonishing invasion of the supernatural."

John Bosco experienced a life-shaping dream in 1824, when he was only nine years old. He saw himself in a field, surrounded by children who were yelling and fighting. He tried to calm them, first by persuasion, then by force. "Don't use violence," said a mysterious person. "Be gentle if you want to win their friendship." The children had momentarily transmogrified into wild animals, but now they appeared to become submissive lambs. Then, rising above the scene, a woman's voice instructed John to "take your crook and lead them out to pasture." That dream set the course of his life, and it recurred to lead him at crucial junctions of his life.

A passionate desire to rescue homeless boys consumed John Bosco from his youth. As a young man, he made sporadic efforts to reach out to youths in his neighborhood. His real ministry, however, began in 1841, after his ordination as a priest at Turin, in northern Italy. There he began to gather boys on Sundays for recreation and teaching. Gradually over the next fifteen years, the young priest built an impressive community that cared for the poor youth of Turin.

He worked tirelessly, establishing residence halls, workshops for apprentices, and Latin schools to prepare men for the priesthood. By 1856, 500 boys were attending his Sunday events and 150 were housed with him. Ten young priests staffed four apprentice workshops and four Latin classes. All gathered for worship and study in the church of St. Francis de Sales, which he had constructed for the children in 1852. Thus, Don Bosco followed his dream. ("Don" is the Italian term of address for priests.) He used his extraordinary pastoral gifts to care for his boys as a shepherd cares for his flock.

139

He accomplished all of this against great odds. Landlords, city officials, and Turin's socialites often blocked Don Bosco's way because his filthy, rambunctious boys inconvenienced and frightened them.

Even his fellow clerics gave him trouble. Once, two of his priest friends decided that his fantastic visions were marks of insanity and developed a plot to get him confined to an asylum. The plan was to lure him into a carriage that would carry him off to a mental hospital. The priests arranged for attendants at the asylum to incarcerate, forcibly if necessary, the occupant of the carriage. The priests then visited John Bosco and, after a brief conversation, invited him to take a ride in the country. However, Don Bosco, by divine intuition, had read their scheme perfectly. As he and the others approached the carriage, he politely stepped aside and forced his two friends to get in, slamming the door behind them. "Quick!" he shouted to the driver. "To the asylum. Don't stop till you get there. You've got two dangerous characters locked inside." The driver rushed the priests to the institution, where several husky attendants restrained them. Despite the priests' protests, the aides locked them up for several uncomfortable hours before they discovered the mistake and released them. Never again did the priests try to trick Don Bosco.

To add to his difficulties, Don Bosco had very little money to work with. From his poverty, however, riches seemed to flow. When he had a need, he did everything humanly possible to meet it. Then he counted on God to intervene. And intervene God did, in instances too numerous to mention. Let me give just one representative example.

In 1866, as Don Bosco built the great church of Our Lady, Help of Christians, he regularly ran out of money. One day he needed four thousand francs to pay his contractors. By midmorning, benefactors had contributed one thousand francs. In the afternoon, he wandered the streets, seeking a miracle for the rest. A wealthy man's servant approached him and asked him to visit his master, who had been bedridden for three years. Sensing an opportunity, Don Bosco went to the sick man's bedside.

"Reverend Father," the man said, "I need your prayers. I hurt so much that I can't move at all, and the doctors give me no hope. If I get even a little relief, I'll make a generous donation to your work."

"How fortunate!" said Don Bosco. "Today we need three thousand francs for construction of Our Lady, Help of Christians."

"I couldn't possibly arrange that today," he said. "Besides, I'm too sick to go to the bank."

"And why shouldn't you get up and go to the bank?" asked Don Bosco. "We need the money now. Nothing is impossible to God." Then he rounded up everyone in the house to pray for the man's healing.

With the whole household around him as witnesses, the man recovered instantaneously. He jumped out of bed and asked for his clothes. Dressed for the first time in months, he sat down to a huge lunch with many courses of rich food. Then, delighted to be out of the house, he went to the bank and returned shortly with the three thousand francs.

"I am completely cured," he exclaimed repeatedly.

"You take your money out of the bank," said Don Bosco, "and Our Lady, Help of Christians, takes you out of the bed."

Don Bosco's dedicated service to others also occasioned miracles. In 1854, a cholera epidemic struck Turin. He assigned forty-four of his boys to tend the sick and carry victims to temporary hospitals. The boys worked from October through December, bringing relief to many sick people. Not one of them contracted the highly infectious disease.

A year later, Don Bosco decided to have three hundred juvenile offenders released from their imprisonment in a reformatory so they could spend a day of recreation in a park. He needed to get permission from Urban Ratazzi, the home minister of the country, to do so. Ratazzi was a leading opponent of the church, and Don Bosco hoped to intrigue him with a little miracle. The official feared that many boys might seize the opportunity to escape, but Don Bosco charmed him with many assurances, and finally he allowed the event. The boys had a great time in the open air, with games, sports, a picnic, and ferverinos from the priest, who had quickly become their hero. At the end of the day—to Ratazzi's great surprise—Don Bosco returned like a shepherd with his sheep. Mounted on a donkey and surrounded by a rowdy parade of boys, he had not lost a single one.

141

Don Bosco's supernatural knowledge was the most startling and discomfiting of his miraculous gifts. Contemporaries described his eyes as "penetrating." With a glance he could look into people's souls and read their spiritual state. Over the years, hundreds of boys were moved to repentance when he quietly urged them to confess a secret sin. Once, an incredulous newcomer challenged him before a crowd of boys. "If Don Bosco knows any of my sins, he can tell them aloud," he said. Don Bosco leaned close to the boy's ear and whispered an accurate list of his sins. "You must have heard my confession at church this morning!" exclaimed the surprised youth. "I don't think so!" shouted all the boys. "Don Bosco has been with us the whole day."

In dreams and visions, Don Bosco foresaw the future. At least 150 of the saint's revelatory dreams are a matter of record. A vision of fiery tongues over a boy's head would tell him that the young man was called to the priesthood. On many occasions a dream would reveal to him a colleague's life span or a boy's approaching death. He used the supernatural information to encourage his fellows to persevere through hard times. Whenever he foresaw an impending death, he did all he could to help the person die well. He composed an "exercise for a happy death," which he regularly had his boys recite as a means of focusing them on the serious side of life.

Don Bosco had uncanny revelations of faraway events and situations. In 1886, while he was in Turin, he supernaturally ferreted out a pedophile who was seducing boys many miles away at one of his schools in Barcelona. The priest in charge of the school testified later that Don Bosco had mysteriously appeared to him in a series of dreams and had compelled him to confront and dismiss the man. Astounded and broken by Don Bosco's revelation, the offender confessed his wrongdoing and left the school.

Dreams also guided Don Bosco's work. He foresaw that he would assemble a large company of priests who would extend his ministry to the far ends of the earth. In 1854, he organized a band of his helpers, who took the name Salesians, after Francis de Sales, Don Bosco's favorite saint. The church established the Salesians as a religious community in 1869. By 1875, Don Bosco was sending missionaries as far away as South America. In 1883, an incredible dream revealed to him the future worldwide extent of his communities. In it he envisioned automobiles, airplanes, and freeways as the means of transportation that would connect his widely scattered mission centers! This dream was realized early in the twentieth century, when thousands of Salesians were at work throughout the world.

I would have liked to meet John Bosco in order to watch him first-hand with his boys. Perhaps his supreme generosity would have been contagious and would have awakened a spirit of kindness in me. And I think about how I might have reacted to his spectacular miracles. His supernatural healings would have certainly impressed me, but prompted by my extreme caution, and to my detriment, I probably would have taken a wait-and-see attitude toward his prophecies.

And for sure, I would have avoided looking Don John Bosco in the eye.

Exercise for a Happy Death

143

When my feet, benumbed in death, shall warn me that my mortal course is drawing to a close—Merciful Jesus, have mercy on me!

When my eyes, dim and troubled at the approach of death, shall fix themselves on thee, my last and only support—Merciful Jesus, have mercy on me!

When my ears, soon to be shut forever to the words of men, shall be opened to hear your voice pronouncing the sentence of my irrevocable doom—Merciful Jesus, have mercy on me!

When I shall have lost the use of my senses; when the world shall have vanished from my sight; when my agonizing soul shall feel the sorrow of death—Merciful Jesus, have mercy on me!

St. John Bosco

PART SIX

MIRACLES THAT CHANGED *the* COURSE *of* HISTORY

The saints give little thought to changing the world around them. They are too busy changing the world within them. They are not out to reform Caesar, but to conform themselves to Christ.

CLARE BOOTHE LUCE

ave you ever tried to find God's will for your life? Like me, you may have spent hours searching for wisdom about an important decision. On the whole, I think my time wrestling with this issue of God's will has been time well spent. But when I reflect on the lives of the saints, I wonder if there might be a better way to know the will of God.

Sometimes I devote more energy to looking for God's plan for my life than to looking for God himself. I do believe he has a plan, but not the caricature that I sometimes make of it. Retreat master Martin Smith says that Christians are often mistaken in the way they try to learn God's will. "Do you really believe," he asks, "that God hides his will from us and expects us to search for it as though we are on a treasure hunt?"

Isn't knowing God's will more of a surrender than a search? We give ourselves to God, and the desires of our hearts blend with his. His wanting becomes our wanting, says Martin Smith, and our plans give way to his. Look at the simple obedience of the mystics and the divinely inspired fruit it bore.

Shortly after Ignatius of Loyola gave his life to Christ, he thought the divine will for him was to undertake severe penances and to go barefoot to Jerusalem, where he was to repent for his past sins and evangelize Muslims. However, the more he surrendered to God, the more he entered into God's real plan. Then he recruited and trained a community of men whose combined service of evangelization and education helped shape the history of the church and the world.

When Francis Xavier said yes to God and no to his own plans, he unexpectedly accomplished something of great historical significance. He spread Christianity to the East, permanently affecting the lives of millions of people. The submission of Francis Xavier and Ignatius of Loyola shows one way God keeps a hand in world events: by using one person's surrender to influence the course of human history.

The same is true for Joan of Arc. The Maid of Orleans's surrender to God put her in the forefront of world events. Where on earth, wondered the leaders of France, did this nineteen-year-old peasant girl get the idea that she should lead an army? The idea, however, did not come from earth. From age twelve, Joan heard voices from heaven that said God wanted her to lead the French to victory. Joan's obedience led her to accomplish a task that seemed humanly impossible. The memory of her still touches the imagination and hearts of millions worldwide, perhaps more than any other saint.

The surrender of the saints gave God permission to intervene directly in human events. That accounts for the flow of signs and wonders in their wakes. You can see this in St. Patrick. As a young man he traded his own wants for God's. What God wanted, it seemed, was the conversion of Ireland to Christianity. Patrick did it in grand style. He upstaged magicians, baptized people, built churches, trained clerics, and educated young people. All the while he was guided by visions and dreams, and miracles swirled about him.

The saints make a pretty strong case for surrender as a strategy for knowing God's will. Maybe it's time to stop searching so hard, in order to let Christ shape our hearts in ways that enable us to both know and do what he wants.

Miraculous Voices

St. Joan of Arc (1412–31)

Nearly all the saints had a "religious" task to perform, and they had to leave the world, so as to be free to accomplish it. But Joan breaks through this rule.

She was called to perform a purely worldly task, to free a people from unendurable political misery, to set a rightful king on the throne, to expel the enemy. She doesn't leave the world because of her mission. Because of it she goes into the world, right into most dangerous places, into the court, into camp, into war.

Ida Coudenhove

The church officially remembers Joan of Arc not as a martyr but as a virgin—the Maid of Orleans. Of course, Joan was a martyr, but not in the technical sense. Yes, she died because she did what she thought God wanted her to do. But she was killed for her politics, not for her faith. Pagans did not execute her for refusing to worship their gods. Infidels did not slay her for defying them. Political enemies burned her at the stake for defeating them at war.

Paradoxically, Christian people, good and bad alike, cheered at her demise. Other Christians wept. This incongruity may trouble us, but Joan would have expected it. The war she fought embroiled French Christians against English Christians. We too have waged wars like that, pitting Christian against Christian. Just as we may have felt that God was on our side, Joan believed that God was with the French. When the judges who condemned her asked if the heavenly voices she followed to war spoke in English, she replied tartly, "Why should they speak English when they were not on the English side?"

Joan of Arc was born into the violent times of the fifteenth century. During her childhood, King Henry V of England invaded France and seized Normandy. He laid claim to the crown of the French king, Charles VI, who was mentally ill. Paralyzed by civil war between the duke of Burgundy and the duke of Orleans, the French could not put up much of a defense. Things worsened when

149

agents of the duke of Orleans murdered the duke of Burgundy. The Burgundians reacted by becoming England's allies.

Eventually, Burgundian mercenaries brought the war home to Joan's family. The raiders sacked the little village of Domrémy-la-Pucelle, forcing them to flee. Thus, the indiscriminate brutality of war disrupted Joan of Arc's pleasant childhood to acquaint her with fear.

Both the English king and the French king died in 1422, but their successors pursued the war. The English, with Burgundian support, marched steadily across France, taking one town at a time. Charles VII, the heir to the French throne, was not yet crowned or anointed king. The enemy controlled the road to Reims, the traditional site where French kings were crowned. Regarding the situation as hopeless, the future king languished with his court near Orleans.

In 1424, when Joan was only twelve years old, the great miracle of her life unfolded. One summer day in her father's garden, she heard a mysterious voice, which was accompanied by a bright light. "At first I was very much frightened," she said later. "The voice came toward the hour of noon. I had fasted the preceding day. I heard the voice on my right hand, in the direction of the church. I seldom hear it without seeing a light. The light always appears on the side from which I hear the voice."

She identified the speaker as Michael the Archangel. Subsequently, he spoke to her many times, gradually revealing a preposterous mission. "You have been chosen to restore the kingdom of France," said the voice, "and to protect King Charles." She was to accomplish these things as the head of the army! Imagine the terror and confusion the archangel's messages must have caused young Joan.

Michael also told her that St. Catherine and St. Margaret would appear to her. God was sending these saints, he said, so she must obey their directions. Over the next seven years, Michael, Catherine, and Margaret are said to have visited Joan frequently, sometimes several times a day. Not only could she see and hear her heavenly messengers, but she could also touch and smell them. At her trial she testified that she physically embraced the saints and that they had a pleasant fragrance.

Joan found the visions comforting, but they also put her under great stress. Fear of her strict father compelled her to keep them secret; she confided only in her parish priest. The messages must have both thrilled and troubled her. The revelations conflicted with reality. How would a simple pleasant girl accomplish such imposing, if not impossible, tasks?

By May 1428, Joan's voices had become relentless and specific. They directed her to go at once to a town nearby and to offer her services to Robert de Baudricourt, the commander of the royal forces. Reluctantly, she obeyed. De Baudricourt, however, greeted her with laughter, telling her that her father should give her a good spanking.

At that time, conditions were deteriorating for the French. The English had put Orleans under siege, and the stronghold was in grave danger. Joan's voices became more insistent. "But I am merely a girl! I cannot ride a horse or wield a weapon!" she protested.

"It is God who commands it!" came the reply.

Unable to resist any longer, Joan secretly made her way back to de Baudricourt. When she arrived she told the commander a fact she could have known only by revelation. She said the French army—on that very day—had suffered a defeat near Orleans. Joan urged him to send her to Orleans so that she might fulfill her mission. When official reports confirmed Joan's word, de Baudricourt finally took her seriously and sent her to Charles VII.

Charles kept Joan waiting three days before he admitted her to court. When Joan entered, the king was in disguise, hiding among his courtiers. But Joan went directly to him. The voices had given her a secret sign, and when she communicated it to Charles, it convinced him of her authenticity. Pressed by suspicious advisers, he had a team of theologians examine Joan at Poitiers. They discerned no problems and recommended that Charles make judicious use of her services.

Thus the way was cleared for Joan of Arc to fulfill her divinely appointed task. She was outfitted with white armor and provided a special standard bearing the names Jesus and Mary. The banner depicted two kneeling angels offering a fleur-de-lis to God. On April 29, 1429, Joan led her army into Orleans. Miraculously, she rallied the town. By May 8, the French had captured the English forts and had lifted the siege. An arrow had penetrated the armor over Joan's breast, but the injury was not serious enough to keep her out of the battle. Everything, including the wound, occurred exactly as Joan had prophesied before the campaign. A peasant maiden had defeated the army of a mighty kingdom, a humiliation that demanded revenge.

The way to Reims was now open. Joan urged the immediate coronation of the king, but the French leaders dragged their feet. Finally, however, at Reims on July 17, 1429, Charles VII was anointed king of France. The Maid of Orleans stood triumphantly at his side. Joan had accomplished her mission.

During the battles at Orleans, the voices had told Joan she had only a little time left. Her shameful end lurked ominously in the shadows. Later, she sustained a serious arrow wound in the thigh during an unsuccessful attack on Paris. In May 1430, after spending the winter in court, she led a force to relieve Compiègne, which the Burgundians had under siege. Her effort failed, and the Burgundians captured her.

Through the summer and fall, the duke of Burgundy held Joan captive. The French, apparently ungrateful, made no effort to rescue her or obtain her release. On November 21, 1430, the Burgundians sold Joan to the English for a large sum. The English were quite eager to punish the maiden who had bested them.

They could not execute Joan for winning, but they could impose capital punishment for sorcery or heresy. For several months she was chained in a cell in the castle at Rouen, where five coarse guards constantly taunted her. In February 1431, Joan appeared before a tribunal headed by Peter Cauchon, the avaricious and wicked bishop of Beauvais.

Joan had no chance for a fair trial. She stood alone before devious judges, an uneducated girl conducting her own defense. The panel interrogated her six times in public, nine times in private. They questioned her closely about her visions, voices, male dress, faith, and submissiveness to the church. Giving good, sometimes even unexpectedly clever answers, Joan handled herself courageously. However, the judges took advantage of her lack of education and tripped her up on a few slippery theological points. The panel packed its summary with her damaging replies and condemned her with that unfair report. They declared that demons inspired her revelations.

The tribunal decided that unless Joan recanted, she was to die as a heretic. At first she refused. But later, when she was taken before a huge throng, she seems to have made some sort of retraction. When she was returned to prison, however, somehow she was tricked into wearing men's clothing, which she had promised to forsake.

Cauchon visited her, observed her dress, and determined that she had fallen back into error. Joan, her strength renewed, then repudiated her earlier retraction. She declared that God had truly commissioned her and that her voices had come from him. "Be of good cheer!" Cauchon said to an English lord as he left the castle. "We'll get her yet!" Cauchon reported these events to the tribunal. On his word, on May 29, 1431, having condemned Joan of Arc as a relapsed heretic, the judges remanded her to the state for execution. The next morning she was taken into Rouen's public square and burned at the stake.

Like Jesus' life, Joan of Arc's life seemed to end in failure.

Twenty-three years later, however, Joan's mother and brothers asked that her case be reopened. Pope Callistus III appointed a commission to review the matter. In 1456, the new panel repudiated the trial and verdict and completely restored Joan's reputation. Once again her piety and exemplary conduct had triumphed.

Few Christians hear heaven-sent voices. I know I don't. Joan was one of those rare exceptions who did. She obeyed what she perceived to be God's directions, and against all odds she achieved the purpose she was given. Though I've never heard a heaven-sent voice, now and then I sense something God wants of me. Doesn't that also happen to you? Perhaps Joan's example will reach down through the centuries to encourage us to listen closely for and to obey God's message to us.

The Death of St. Joan

And when they had come into the market square there was a great concourse of many thousands awaiting them, and in the midst was a heap of mortar very high, hardened to stone, and a tall stake standing in it, and the faggots piled around it. These, after one deputed had preached at her, she mounted without faltering, and was chained to the stake. But being there, above the people, and seen by all, she forgave her enemies and begged each priest in that multitude to say one Mass for her soul.

Then she asked for a cross, and an English soldier bound two sticks together and held it up for her to take, which she kissed and put into the bosom of her white robe. She asked also for a crucifix from the church at hand, and this was found and given her. And when she had held this up before her and kissed it also fervently, while the English lords clamored at the delay, the torch was set to the faggots, and in the midst of the smoke they heard her proclaiming firmly that indeed her mission was of God, and they heard her praying to the saints; till, in a very little while, a loud voice came from the midst of the burning, the holy name Jesus, called so loudly that every man heard it to the very ends of the square. And after that there was silence, and no sound but the crackling of the fire.

Hilaire Belloc

Miracles over Magic

ST. PATRICK (C. 389–C. 461)

Ireland, which never had the knowledge of God, but up till now always adored idols and things unclean—how are they now made a people of the Lord, and are called children of God? The sons of the Scots and the daughters of their chieftains are seen to become monks and virgins of Christ.

ST. PATRICK

Our family wears green on St. Patrick's Day or else we answer to the lady of the house. Her March 17 excesses have included making perfectly good food unpalatable with green dye. Sometimes I think my dear Irish wife's blood must run emerald.

I wonder what Patrick himself would make of the shenanigans that mark his feast day in the United States. Would he be comfortable with the festivities of his annual commemoration? Would he wear a shamrock? wield a shillelagh? dance a jig? recite limericks? eat green food and drink green beer?

I will not say that Patrick would not enjoy all that hoopla. After all, historians call him the first true Irishman. So we can expect that, like his compatriots, he knew how to celebrate. Perhaps, however, Patrick would like to see us enhance his day of remembrance with some specifically Christian customs, as many do in Ireland. Like taking time out to pray or to study the Bible or to share a word of faith with a neighbor. For prayer, study, and evangelism were the real hallmarks of his life.

Patrick first came to Ireland as a slave in 405, when raiders tore him and many others from their homes in Roman Britain. For six years, near a mountain in northern Ireland, Patrick herded swine for his pagan master. In his *Confession,* he says that his bondage was a time of spiritual strengthening. "My love and fear of God," he said, "increased greatly, and my faith grew, and my spirit was stirred up."

155

He spent his days and his nights praying. "Before dawn, in snow and frost and rain, I used to be aroused to prayer," he recalled. "Nor was there any tepidity in me, such as I now feel, because then the spirit was fervent within me."

One night, Patrick heard a heavenly voice in his dreams that revealed he would soon return to his homeland. Later on, the voice spoke of a ship two hundred miles away that would carry him to Britain. Patrick fled from his master and walked the long distance to the boat. When he arrived, the captain at first refused to take him. After Patrick prayed, however, the captain reconsidered and gave him passage.

The ship reached shore in three days. Then Patrick and the sailors trekked for a month through rough terrain. When their food ran out, the shipmaster challenged him to pray to his God for help. "Turn earnestly," said Patrick, "and with all your hearts to the Lord my God, to whom nothing is impossible." Just then a herd of swine appeared on the road, and the pigs soon became a hearty barbecue. Until Patrick left the seamen a month later, they did not lack for food or anything else.

Patrick was about twenty-two years old when he rejoined his family. They welcomed him warmly, hoping he would never again leave them. But that was not to be. He soon received dreams that urged him to return to Ireland. "I heard," he wrote, "the voices of those who dwelt beside the wood of Focluth, which is by the western sea. And thus they cried, as if with one mouth: 'We beg you, holy youth, to come and walk once more among us.'" Patrick understood that God was calling him to take the gospel to Ireland. In fact, to become the Apostle of Ireland.

Patrick went to France, where he worked for twenty-one years preparing for his mission. Establishing the Christian church in Ireland would require many things. He would have to be ready to proclaim the Good News to a pagan people. He would have to be able to provide for the Christian formation and care of his converts.

Wherever he founded communities, he would need to recruit and train a native clergy and build and equip churches. Above all, he would have to possess the strength and savvy to overcome the resistance of the druids, the priests who used magic to dominate the Irish.

For three years, Patrick devoted himself to acquiring spiritual disciplines and practical skills at the monastery of Lérins. Then he spent fifteen more at Auxerre, where the great monk and bishop St. Germanus was his mentor. Patrick's training prepared him to be a church planter, not a scholar. Later, he keenly felt his lack of education and often bemoaned it. However, he knew that for his task he needed pastoral wisdom more than scholarship. During this time, Patrick was ordained a deacon and a priest. Ireland's first bishop, St. Palladius, died in 431 after only one year of service. Patrick succeeded him as bishop and launched his divinely appointed enterprise in 432.

The pivotal event in St. Patrick's ministry occurred in the spring of 433. He was determined to win the support of High-King Laoghaire, the powerful ruler of central Ireland, whose blessing would open doors for him everywhere. His resolve to gain the king's support precipitated a dramatic confrontation with leading druids. Patrick's triumph over them in a contest of spiritual power versus magic secured the success of his mission at its outset.

It happened on the night before Easter. Laoghaire was celebrating a pagan festival at Tara, his base in central Ireland. By law, no one in the land was permitted to kindle a fire until the ceremonial beacon on Royal Hill was lit. Miles away atop the Hill of Slane, Patrick had gathered his followers for the Easter Vigil. Unaware of the prohibition against fires, Patrick opened the liturgy by striking the new fire, the vivid symbol of Christ's resurrection. Had he known of the prohibition, he probably would have ignored it anyway.

King Laoghaire, his barons, and the druids saw Patrick's paschal fire and were enraged. The druids, sensing imminent danger, warned the king that he must extinguish the fire immediately. If not, said one prophetically, "it will never be extinguished in Ireland. Moreover, it will outshine all the fires we light. And he who has kindled it will conquer us all." So the king and eight chariots full of warriors headed for Patrick's camp.

Upon arrival the king summoned Patrick and demanded an explanation. Patrick responded with a simple summary of the gospel. When Drochu, a leading druid, made fun of the Christian mysteries, Patrick prayed aloud that he be punished. With that, Drochu was swooped high into the air and dropped to his death. The warriors then attempted to capture Patrick, but he prayed they would be scattered. A dark cloud and a whirlwind descended on them, causing a panic in which many perished.

The king cowered at this demonstration of might. In his fright, he made a pretense of acknowledging God and invited Patrick to speak about the Christian faith to his barons at Tara. Then he left Slane, planning to lie in wait to ambush Patrick and his associates. When Patrick and his band passed by, however, they were invisible to Laoghaire and his would-be assassins. As the Christians escaped, they chanted for the first time the saint's famous Breastplate. The prayer calls upon the power of the Trinity, the Incarnation, the angels, and all of heaven against every conceivable danger. In the following years, Patrick would pray it often.

On Easter day, King Laoghaire held a banquet at Tara as part of the pagan religious festival. Patrick and five companions mystified the gathering by passing through locked doors and appearing in their midst. Invited to sit near the king, Patrick was then given a drink that Lucat-Mael, the chief druid, had laced with poison. Discerning the mischief, Patrick made a sign of the cross over the cup, and the beverage froze, except for the drop of poison. Everyone watched as Patrick poured it on the table. He blessed the cup again, and his drink returned to normal.

After this humiliation before his peers, Lucat-Mael sought to redeem himself. He challenged Patrick to a public contest of wonders on the plain of Tara, where many Irish could watch. First, the druid is said to have magically filled the plain with waist-high snow.

"We see the snow," said Patrick. "Now, remove it."

"I cannot until tomorrow," said the druid.

"Then, you are powerful for evil, but not for good. Not so with me," said Patrick. He stretched out his hands, once again carving a cross in the air. Instantly, the snow disappeared without a trace. The crowd cheered.

For his next magical stunt, the druid shrouded the plain in total darkness. Once again he was unable to reverse his trick until the next day. Patrick prayed and with a blessing dismissed the darkness. This time, the onlookers erupted with praise for Patrick's God.

To settle the issue once and for all, Patrick proposed the third contest, a trial by fire. The druid, covered by Patrick's cloak, would be locked in a hut made of freshly sawed wood. Benignus, Patrick's young disciple, would be clothed in Lucat-Mael's cloak and placed in a hut of dry wood. Then both huts would be burned to the ground. All accepted the terms, and with the two men in place, the huts were torched. This test had a marvelous outcome. Flames consumed the hut of new wood and the druid, but Patrick's cloak was not even singed. Benignus and his hut remained untouched by the fire, but Lucat-Mael's cloak was burned to ashes.

Patrick's miraculous encounters with the druids were so spectacular that modern historians discount them as legends. But as extraordinary as the miracles were, the earliest documents reported them as facts. Patrick's wonders set the stage for the conversion of Ireland. Why should he not have expected divine interventions at such significant moments in his missionary venture?

159

Even though Patrick had exposed the emptiness of Laoghaire's religion, the ruler did not become a Christian. He made two decisions, however, that significantly advanced Patrick's work. He gave Patrick permission to preach the gospel in Ireland, and he ensured Patrick's personal safety.

From that time, Patrick crisscrossed the island, making disciples everywhere he went. In a relatively short time, he baptized tens of thousands of converts and built hundreds of churches, staffing them with Irish priests and deacons. He founded many monasteries and schools to care for the passionate youths who decided to follow him to Christ. In 444, scarcely a dozen years after Patrick arrived, he established Ireland's first cathedral church at Armagh, which quickly became a center of Christian education and church administration.

By the time of Patrick's death around 461, he had completely dislodged the ancient paganism. The whole island had become thoroughly and permanently Christian. Now that's a miracle I challenge anyone to dismiss.

Christ Is All in All

Christ with me, Christ before me,
Christ behind me, Christ within me,
Christ beneath me, Christ above me,
Christ at my right, Christ at my left.

Christ in the head of everyone who thinks of me,
Christ in the mouth of everyone who speaks to me,
Christ in every eye that sees me,
Christ in every ear that hears me.

St. Patrick's Breastplate

Miracles of Discernment and Obedience
St. Ignatius of Loyola (1491–1556)

Unless the LORD builds the house,
*   its builders labor in vain.*

PSALM 127:1

Twenty-twenty hindsight about the saints may mislead us. We look back at these near-finished products and imagine that they dropped out of the womb in a state of perfect holiness, candidates for canonization. But only immaculately conceived Mary fits that description, and even she suffered under the weight of our humanness. Like the saints and all of us, she had to grow in faith and discipleship.

Or we may survey the saints' accomplishments and jump to false conclusions. Admiration for the achievements of great religious orders may cause us to misconstrue the intent and actions of their founders. Francis and Dominic, for example, did not put the Friars Minor and the Friars Preachers on rails to roar through the centuries generating global spiritual renewal. They simply set out to follow Christ. In their enthusiasm they made some mistakes along the way. When the Lord told Francis to rebuild his church, he repaired the church of St. Damian. Dominic thought he was supposed to evangelize the Tartars in Russia but wound up preaching to the Albigensians in southern France. Francis and Dominic eventually succeeded because they obeyed Christ, and he took them where he wanted them to go. Who knows what they would have achieved had they merely followed their own inclinations.

161

That was also the case with St. Ignatius of Loyola. After his conversion in 1521, he wanted only to repent of his sins with harsh penances and to go to Jerusalem to convert Muslims. Later he came to see his mission as helping others meet God and find their place in the divine plan. However, even after he had assembled a small circle of devoted companions in the 1530s, he did not conceive of consolidating them into an army for Christ. Only in 1539, nearly two decades after his conversion, did the Holy Spirit and circumstances prompt Ignatius to organize the Society of Jesus as a religious order.

Had you known Ignatius of Loyola, you might have predicted his success at whatever he decided to do. You would have recognized his steely determination to complete whatever he had begun, a quality he inherited from his Basque ancestors. "He has already driven the nail," a Roman cardinal once said of his obstinacy. You also would have noticed Ignatius's other Basque characteristics—his meditative spirit, his measured speech, and his fearlessness.

However, you might not have guessed that Ignatius would become a mystic and a saint. He had received the tonsure of a cleric as a youth but had no intention of pursuing a religious life. Instead he dreamed of a romantic future as a knight at the royal court. Like other young Spanish nobles, he was known to go drinking with his comrades and to flirt with attractive women. His bravado sometimes got him into trouble. Once, Ignatius was arrested for instigating a brawl with the parish clergy of Loyola. Only his clerical status prevented his being prosecuted in civil court on very serious charges. "Although he was attached to the faith," said one of his close friends, "his life was in no way conformed to it nor did he keep himself free from sin. Rather he was particularly reckless in gambling, in his dealings with women, in quarreling, and with the sword."

In 1521, everything began to change for Ignatius. In May of that year, the French invaded Spain, moving with superior forces through Navarre toward Castile. Only the fortress at Pamplona stood in their way. Ignatius had led a small volunteer army to Pamplona's defense and had galvanized the citadel's dispirited forces against their imminent defeat. During an artillery battle on May 23, Ignatius fought courageously until a cannonball passed between his legs, shattering the right one and wounding the left. With the hero of Pamplona down, the battle ended quickly and the fortress surrendered. From that moment Ignatius's life took a different course, a gradual but dramatic transformation.

Out of respect for his valor, the French treated Ignatius honorably and had him carried by litter to Loyola. Because his leg was not healing correctly, doctors rebroke and reset it. He endured the procedure in a knightly manner, not complaining but clenching his fists, the only admission of pain that the chivalric code allowed. However, the operation left Ignatius in a grievously weakened condition. On June 28, the eve of the feast of Sts. Peter and Paul, doctors told him that unless he improved by midnight, he would die. Ignatius prayed to St. Peter for healing, promising to devote himself to the saint's service. Miraculously, by midnight his condition got better, and he was out of danger.

But Ignatius's ordeal was not over. A bone protruded from his right leg as it began to knit together, and out of vanity he made the doctors saw it off. Again he bore the excruciating pain silently. His physicians tried to stretch the leg so that it would not be shorter than the other, but they failed. For the rest of his life, Ignatius would walk with a slight limp, which he sometimes corrected by wearing a shoe with an elevated heel.

To occupy his mind during his months of recovery, Ignatius requested something to read. As a youth he had become addicted to medieval romances that told of knights who devoted their exploits to highborn ladies, and he hoped for some of these books to entertain him. But the only available books were Ludolph of Saxony's *Life of Christ,* which laced the Gospels with chivalric values, and Jacob of Voragine's *The Golden Legend*, which presented some of the saints as knights in service of Christ the King.

163

At first these books did not appeal to Ignatius, but gradually he became fascinated with the idealism of their heroes. As he meditated on them he wondered, "What if I were to do as St. Francis and St. Dominic did?" He alternated these reflections with romantic reveries of imagined love for an unnamed and probably unattainable lady. These musings taught Ignatius a lesson in discernment: he noticed that thoughts of the lady left him distressed, but thoughts of the saints calmed his soul. He concluded that the devil inspired his worldly dreams and that God inspired his admiration for the saints. This realization occasioned Ignatius's decision to follow Christ. In imitation of the saints, he resolved that in order to repent of his sins he would perform extreme penances and make a pilgrimage to Jerusalem.

One night as Ignatius lay awake, a vision of the Blessed Mother and the child Jesus confirmed his resolution to become a disciple. When he wrote about it years later, he did not reveal the content of the apparition, saying only that it consoled him for a long time and caused recollection of past sexual sins to revolt him. But the vision changed him noticeably; his friends thought he seemed like a different person.

History does not remember Ignatius of Loyola as a wonder-worker. However, a steady stream of divine interventions nudged him along the way to fulfilling God's design for his life. Mystical consolations and visions supported him shortly after his conversion and later when he was gathering companions in Christ's service.

The most memorable of these graces touched Ignatius in 1522 at Manresa while he was en route to Jerusalem. Over several months he experienced a series of intuitions that would remain with him all his life, inspiring his thought and prayer. Once, he sensed an image of the way in which God had created the world, but he said he could not explain what he saw. Another time, during the elevation of the host at Mass, he saw with his inner eyes rays of light that showed him how Christ is present in the Eucharist.

Once, while praying the Little Office of the Blessed Virgin, Ignatius perceived the Trinity as three keys on a musical instrument. This insight affected him so profoundly that he wept copiously. Forty years later Ignatius said that this vision at Manresa shaped his devotion to God and that prayer to the Trinity, especially at Mass, always brought consolations to his soul and tears of joy to his eyes.

An extraordinary mystical experience capped all the others and had a permanent effect on Ignatius's spiritual journey. One day on his way to Mass, he sat down beside the Cardoner River. While gazing at the water, an all-encompassing insight flooded his mind. Many years later he described the event, writing in the third person:

> As he sat, the eyes of his understanding began to open. He beheld no vision, but saw and understood many things, spiritual as well as

those concerning faith and learning. This took place with so great an illumination that these things appeared to be something altogether new. . . . This was so great that in the whole course of his past life right up to his sixty-second year, if he were to gather all the helps he had received from God, and everything he knew, and add them together, he does not think that they would equal all that he received at that one time.

As Ignatius matured in the spiritual life, he developed the ability to discern the source of his mystical phenomena and of his spiritual leadings. He learned to distinguish between consolations that God sent to guide him and those the devil used to sidetrack him. For instance, at Manresa Ignatius often delighted in a vision of a serpent-like object covered with glowing eyes. But shortly after his enlightenment at the Cardoner, while he knelt in thanksgiving before a cross, the thing appeared to him stripped of its beauty. He discerned that the device, which had pleased him so much, was an apparition of the Evil One, and he drove it away with contempt. Later when he was a student, he refused consolations that interrupted his sleep or distracted him from his studies because he recognized that they came from the devil.

Ignatius also discovered that he had mistaken some of his inclinations as leadings from God. For example, after his conversion he thought his life's calling was to imitate the saints' extreme asceticism. However, at Manresa he observed that his excessive fasting, sleep deprivation, going barefoot and without warm clothing, and other practices had weakened his body and plunged him into depression. In the months after his mystical experience by the river, he realized that his real vocation was not asceticism but evangelization. He recognized that God wanted him to share his spiritual experiences with others, praying with them and encouraging them to give their lives to Christ.

Ignatius had already prepared himself for this mission. While recuperating at Loyola, he had begun to make notes on everything he learned from his reading of Scripture and his personal journey. As he accumulated his wisdom on discipleship and discernment, he shaped it into a message that he could present to others. Over the years Ignatius developed these notes into his classic work, *The Spiritual Exercises.*

During the decade after 1524, while pursuing his education at universities in Barcelona, Alcalá, Salamanca, and Paris, Ignatius devoted himself to friendship evangelism. At each school he led a few friends, one-by-one, through a primitive version of the Spiritual Exercises. Through Ignatius's efforts, the Holy Spirit set the lives of these young men on fire with passion for serving the Lord and the gospel. The exercises led them to repent for their sins, to turn to Christ, and to find their place in the divine plan of salvation. Among these friends were Peter Faber and Francis Xavier, themselves future saints.

HUNGRY FOR GOD
Thomas Dubay, S.J.

> Each of us is an incarnated puzzle, and each of us has an insatiable thirst for the infinite. Never content with the limited nibbles and tastes offered by created realities, we find buried in our depths a dynamic that is restless and voracious. Even the self-avowed atheist is, in his or her endless desires, a witness to this basic need for the divine.
>
> Though Jesus shared in none of our wounded sinfulness, his actions as well as his words pointed to the primacy of immersion in the Father. "In the morning, long before dawn, he . . . went off to a lonely place and prayed there. . . . He went off into the hills to pray. . . . He would always go off to some place where he could be alone and pray. . . . He went out into the hills to pray. . . . He was praying alone. . . . He . . . would spend the night on the hill . . ." Mark 1:35; 6:46; Luke 5:16; 6:12; 9:18; 21:37 (JB).

On August 14, 1534, Ignatius and six early companions met at the chapel of St. Denis on the hill of Montmartre in Paris. Peter Faber, the only priest among them, celebrated Mass. Afterward they all vowed to go to the Holy Land to proclaim the gospel to the Muslims. But if circumstances prevented their going to Jerusalem, they promised to offer themselves in service to the pope so that he might deploy them as he wished. Mutual love had drawn the seven together into an informal community that the meeting at St. Denis formalized, but they had yet to think of founding a new religious order.

Ignatius and his companions had hoped to embark for Jerusalem from Venice in 1537, but the Turks controlled the eastern Mediterranean, blocking all travel to the Holy Land. In October 1537, they decided to wait a year for passage to the East, and if that failed, they would fulfill their vow to serve the pope. Then they scattered to university towns to evangelize students. In order to give themselves an identity, they agreed that they would call themselves the Company of Jesus. In the meantime, Ignatius had been ordained a priest, and all seven had taken vows of poverty and chastity. The new name and the vows moved them closer to the formation of a religious community, but they still were not quite there.

By October 1538, Ignatius and his little company realized that they would never get to Jerusalem. So they decided to rendezvous in Rome and present themselves to the pope. On his way to Rome, Ignatius stopped to pray at a dilapidated chapel at La Storta. He was overcome with a desire to ask God for a grace he had wanted since his stay at Manresa. In his memoir, Ignatius says he asked Mary to place him with Jesus so that the Lord might receive him under his standard and accept him totally into his companionship. As Ignatius prayed, in his mind's eye he saw Christ bearing his cross and the Father behind him saying to Christ, "I want you to accept this person as your servant." Jesus accepted Ignatius, saying, "I want you to serve us." Deeply moved by this experience, he received it as divine approval for the work he and his companions were undertaking.

Around November 21, 1538, Ignatius and his associates knelt before Pope Paul III and pledged to serve him and the church. "Why go to Jerusalem?" he said to Ignatius, who still harbored that desire. "Italy is a true Jerusalem," said the pope, "if you want to produce fruit in God's church." Over the next six months he began to deploy them to several Italian cities.

This scattering precipitated the foundation of the Society of Jesus as a new religious order. It forced Ignatius and his disciples to decide whether they would act independently or as a community. They pursued this question with a series of prayerful discussions from March through June 1539, when they finally agreed that they wanted to form a permanent association. They decided to establish an institute under a leader to whom they would vow obedience. Ignatius sketched out their proposed pattern of life: the Society of Jesus was to advance the faith by teaching, preaching, hearing confessions, caring for the sick and imprisoned, and other charitable works. They would embrace evangelical poverty, relying on the Lord to supply all their needs. Every member of the community was to submit under unqualified obedience to Pope Paul III and his successors.

Rome solemnly confirmed the establishment of the society on September 17, 1540. The companions elected Ignatius as the first superior. Out of humility and conviction of his sinfulness, he refused the office until his confessor warned him that he was resisting the Holy Spirit.

From 1541 until his death in 1556, Ignatius governed the Jesuits from Rome. With great care to follow the leadings of the Spirit, he wrote the constitution for the new religious order. While he rooted the company's rule of life on the practice of earlier religious orders, he installed innovations in their life pattern that allowed them to respond effectively to the needs of the times. For example, he did not require members to pray the Liturgy of the Hours in common, wanting them to have enough flexibility to perform their service of education and evangelism. Also, because abuse of ascetical practices had ruined his own health, Ignatius banned extreme fasting and excessive use of other spiritual disciplines.

You must understand how small the Jesuit beginnings were. Put yourself in Ignatius's shoes. He had no idea where the Spirit would lead his community. Only ten men constituted the new religious order, and at first Rome limited their growth to sixty. In 1541, no one dreamed that before the end of the sixteenth century hundreds of Jesuits would lead the Catholic Reformation, spread the church to the East from India to Japan, and establish universities that would influence millions in the future.

On two occasions Jesus multiplied a little bread and a few fish to feed thousands. I think that was a model of the miracle he works with people. He takes a few people like Ignatius and his companions and multiplies them to build and refresh his church. I think we should all aspire to be like the little boy who provided the bread and fish for Jesus' miracle. We should offer ourselves and our gifts to him and watch for the miracles he works in and through us.

Purpose and Choices

Man is created to praise, reverence, and serve God our Lord, and by this means to save his soul. All other things on the face of the earth are created for man to help him fulfill the end for which he is created. From this it follows that man is to use these things to the extent that they will help him to attain his end. Likewise, he must rid himself of them in so far as they prevent him from attaining it.

Therefore we must make ourselves indifferent to all created things, in so far as it is left to the choice of our free will and is not forbidden. Acting accordingly, for our part, we should not prefer health to sickness, riches to poverty, honor to dishonor, a long life to a short one. And so in all things we should desire and choose only those things that will best help us attain the end for which we are created.

St. Ignatius of Loyola

A Miracle Within

ST. FRANCIS XAVIER (1506–52)

If anyone would come after me, he must deny himself and take up his cross and follow me. For whoever wants to save his life will lose it, but whoever loses his life for me and for the gospel will save it.

MARK 8:34–35

Francis Xavier had planned to devote himself to the intellectual life, but at a strategic moment he surrendered to God, who had long and patiently pursued him. That surrender changed the course of his life—and the course of history as well. Even Ignatius of Loyola, the leader of the new Jesuit community, had planned to deploy Francis as a scholar. But India beckoned, and Ignatius reluctantly sent Francis to preach the gospel there. Thus, the man who had planned on a leisurely intellectual life became a missionary apostle, perhaps second only to St. Paul.

In 1525, Francis left Xavier, his mother's castle near Pamplona in Navarre, to study at the University of Paris. He enrolled at the College of St. Barbara, where he pursued an unwaveringly successful academic career. Within three short years he had earned his degree and was lecturing in philosophy. At St. Barbara, circumstances put Xavier's spiritual career on course. Through his roommate, St. Peter Faber, Francis became a friend of Ignatius of Loyola. This relationship gradually revolutionized his life.

Ignatius had experienced a radical conversion to Christ and had devoted his life to helping others in their spiritual quests. He challenged his friends to yield their lives to Christ, abandon their own plans, and follow the Lord's design for their lives. Although Francis felt drawn to Ignatius's ideals, he was reluctant to make them his own. He resisted Ignatius's magnetic influence for six years because it threatened the comfortable life he wanted as a church-supported scholar.

⌇

One day in 1533, however, things came to a crisis. The cathedral of Pamplona in Navarre had just appointed Francis a canon with a secure income. As he reflected on his dream come true, he overheard Loyola and Peter Faber discussing their plans in the next room. At that moment Francis mysteriously felt all his resistance to Ignatius slip away. A desire to throw in with Loyola captivated Xavier's heart and dismissed his own life plan.

As Francis reached his decision, the text of Genesis 12:1 crossed his mind: "Leave your country, your people and your father's household and go to the land I will show you." That verse gave him a prophetic inkling of the unanticipated direction his life would take.

In 1534, Francis Xavier was among the first seven men to decide to formally join Ignatius of Loyola's community. They were the first Jesuits, and Francis was ordained a priest three years later. Loyola had long-term plans to deploy Xavier as a scholar and teacher, but circumstances derailed them. From the beginning, the Jesuits were in high demand, and Ignatius had to scramble to meet all the requests. King John III of Portugal asked for six men to do missionary work in the Portuguese territories in India. Ignatius said he could spare two: Simon Rodriguez and Nicholas Bobadilla, who were to sail to Goa in 1541. At the last moment, however, Bobadilla became seriously ill. With some hesitance and uneasiness, Ignatius asked Francis to go in Bobadilla's place. Thus, Xavier accidentally began his life as an apostle to the East.

⌇

Francis Xavier believed no one was more ill-equipped than he to take the gospel overseas. But he was wrong. En route from Lisbon to Goa, Francis already displayed the cheerfulness and generosity that would become the trademarks of his work. Through his personal charm, he made friends with the toughest seamen on the ship. Then he engaged them in "apostolic conversations," seeking to win them for Christ.

Aboard ship he served others so tirelessly that, exhausted, he became dangerously ill himself. But he would not heed doctors' warnings to take care of himself. Once, he put a delirious and dying sailor in his own bed and lay down himself on a plank. Later, he was found conversing with the man, who had miraculously recovered his senses as soon as he was put into Francis's bed. The sailor died that evening, after confessing his sins and receiving Holy Communion. "His good end," said one observer, "caused the Father great happiness. Indeed, he always looked happy, no matter what his sufferings and burdens."

Xavier arrived in India in 1542. For the next decade he labored selflessly to plant the seeds of Christianity over thousands of miles from Goa to as far as Kyoto, Japan. He died in 1552 while trying to smuggle himself into China, which was closed to missionaries.

Francis's missionary methods were primitive. When he arrived in a village, he rang a bell to summon the children and the idle. He taught them the Apostles' Creed, the Ten Commandments, the Our Father, and other common prayers. Using little songs that the children loved to sing, he instructed them in Christian doctrine. These songs caught on with other villagers, spreading Francis's message. Then, when people expressed simple faith in the creed, he baptized them.

Some believe that Francis Xavier had a miraculous gift of languages, which enabled him to communicate fluently with everyone, but that was not the case. Francis struggled with foreign languages and was barely able to express the creed, commandments, and prayers in Tamil and other native languages. He had to rely on impromptu interpreters and translators, so he was never completely sure he had accurately communicated his message. The real miracle of tongues was that Xavier spread the gospel so far and to so many with such little grasp of their languages.

Miracles of healing, however, occurred frequently in his ministry to poor villages. Once, while traveling through a pagan territory, Francis learned of a woman who had been in labor for three days and was probably near death. Midwives and sorcerers were treating her with superstitious incantations. Xavier went to the woman's home and called on the name of Christ to heal her. "I began with the Creed," he wrote to Ignatius, "which my companion translated into Tamil. By the mercy of God, the woman came to believe in the articles of faith. I asked whether she desired to become a Christian, and she replied that she would most willingly become one. Then I read excerpts from the Gospels in that house where, I think, they were never heard before. I then baptized the woman." As soon as Francis baptized the woman, she was healed and gave birth to a healthy baby.

The woman's family was so touched by this divine intervention that they invited Francis to instruct and baptize all of them, including the newborn. News then traveled quickly throughout the village. A representative of the raja, the overlord, gave the village elders clearance to allow Francis to proclaim Christ there. "First, I baptized the chief men of the place and their families," he wrote, "and afterwards the rest of the people, young and old."

In another village, crowds besieged Francis, begging him to pray for ailing family members. Missionary and teaching duties overwhelmed him, so he enlisted some enthusiastic children to minister to the sick. He sent the children to the homes of the ill and had them gather the family and neighbors. He trained them to proclaim the creed and to assure the sick that if they believed, they would be cured. Thus, Xavier not only responded to requests for prayer, but he managed to spread Christian doctrine throughout the village. Because the sick and their families had faith, he said, "God has shown great mercy to them, healing them in both body and soul." The children of the village had become little miracle workers.

In his passion for spreading the gospel, in his simple obedience, in his humble disregard for himself, the saint was a near perfect imitation of Christ.

Prayer of Surrender

O my God! Teach me to be generous; to give and not to count the cost; to fight and not to heed the wounds; to toil and not to seek for rest; to labor and not to seek for any reward save that of doing your blessed will.

St. Ignatius of Loyola

Afterword

I have noticed an intriguing thread running through the lives of several mystics we have observed. God touched them in extraordinary ways when they prayed the "Veni Creator Spiritus," the ancient hymn to the Holy Spirit.

The hymn is attributed to Rabanus Maurus, a saintly scholar, abbot, and archbishop who lived in ninth-century Germany. The prayer came to be used in the liturgy for Pentecost, and religious communities all over Europe adopted the practice of reciting it.

The "Veni Creator Spiritus" marked the moment when Clare of Assisi made her radical commitment to Christ. St. Francis and his brothers met the lovely runaway at the door of St. Mary of the Angels. As they escorted her to the altar, where she would embrace the gospel, they chanted the beautiful hymn to the Holy Spirit.

If we can believe St. Teresa of Ávila's harsh self-evaluation, her early years as a nun were bogged down in mediocrity. She says her spiritual life only began to flourish when a spiritual director required her to pray daily the "Veni Creator Spiritus." Shortly after Teresa began to pray it, she experienced her first ecstasy. It was as if the hymn opened her spiritual ears to a divine voice within, which seemed to say, "I will not have you hold conversations with men but with angels."

The "Veni Creator Spiritus" also occasioned a deepening of St. Lutgarde's mysticism. Biographer Thomas of Cantimpré reported that one Pentecost, when the hymn was chanted, observers saw Lutgarde mysteriously transported in prayer. They said she appeared to float off the floor. Thomas commented that the saint's body momentarily seemed to share in the supernatural privileges of her spirit, which was elevated heavenward.

Scripture assigns the Holy Spirit the titles of Advocate, Counselor, Helper, Intercessor, and Teacher. He is the One the Father sends to intervene in human lives. He is often depicted as a dove descending gently to us. A line in the "Veni Creator Spiritus" calls him the "finger of God's right hand." Thus, for centuries the church has seen the Spirit as the touch of God in our lives.

Here is the full text of the "Veni Creator Spiritus":

> Come, Creator, Spirit, come
> from your bright heavenly throne,
> come take possession of our souls,
> and make them all your own.
>
> You who are called the Paraclete,
> best gift of God above,
> the living spring, the vital fire,
> sweet christ'ning and true love.
>
> You who are sev'nfold in your grace,
> finger of God's right hand;
> his promise, teaching little ones
> to speak and understand.
>
> O guide our minds with your blest light,
> with love our hearts inflame;
> and with your strength, which ne'er decays,
> confirm our mortal frame.
>
> Far from us drive our deadly foe;
> true peace unto us bring;
> and through all perils lead us safe
> beneath your sacred wing.
>
> Through you may we the Father know,
> through you th' eternal Son,
> and you the Spirit of them both,
> thrice-blessed Three in One.

All glory to the Father be,
with his co-equal Son;
the same to you, great Paraclete,
while endless ages run.

~~~~~~~~

Perhaps this hymn is the best thing you can take away from this book. If we really want to be like the mystics, we won't look for miracles. Nor will we chase after spiritual experiences. Rather, we will let God's Holy Spirit touch our lives.

Saints and Their Feast Days

St. Anthony of Egypt (c. 251–356)	January 17
St. Anthony of Padua (1195–1231)	June 13
St. Apphian (fourth century)	April 2
St. Catherine of Siena (1347–80)	April 29
St. Clare of Assisi (c. 1193–1253)	August 11
St. Dominic (1170–1221)	August 8
St. Elizabeth of Hungary (1207–31)	November 17
St. Francis of Assisi (1181–1226)	October 4
St. Francis of Paola (1416–1507)	April 2
St. Francis Xavier (1506–52)	December 3
St. Gertrude the Great (1256–1302)	November 16
St. Ignatius of Loyola (1491–1556)	July 31
St. Joan of Arc (1412–31)	May 30
St. John Bosco (1815–88)	January 31
St. Lutgarde of Aywières (1182–1246)	June 16
St. Martin de Porres (1579–1639)	November 3
Bl. Padre Pio of Pietrelcina (1887–1968)	September 23
St. Patrick (c. 389–c. 461)	March 17
St. Perpetua (c. 181–203)	March 7
St. Sabas (fourth century)	April 12
Ven. Solanus Casey (1870–1957)	July 31
St. Teresa of Ávila (1515–82)	October 15
St. Theresa Margaret (1747–70)	March 7
St. Vincent Ferrer (c. 1350–1419)	April 5

Bibliography

Allegri, Renzo. *Padre Pio: Man of Hope*. Ann Arbor, Mich.: Servant Publications, 2000.

Angela of Foligno. Complete Works. The Classics of Western Spirituality. Translated by Paul Lachance. New York: Paulist Press, 1993.

Auffray, A., S.D.B. *Saint John Bosco*. Blaisdon, U.K.: Salesian Publications, 1930.

Belloc, Hilaire. *Joan of Arc*. Boston: Little, Brown and Company, 1929.

St. Bonaventure. *The Enkindling Love*. Edited by William I. Joffe. Paterson, N.J.: St. Anthony Guild Press, 1956.

Brady, Ignatius, O.F.M., trans. *The Legend and Writings of Saint Clare of Assisi*. Saint Bonaventure, N.Y.: The Franciscan Institute, 1953.

Brodrick, James, S. J. *Saint Francis Xavier*. New York: Wicklow Press, 1952.

Budge, E. A. Wallis, trans. *The Paradise or Garden of the Holy Fathers*. Seattle: Saint Nectarios Press, 1978.

Bury, J. B. *The Life of St. Patrick and His Place in History*. London: Macmillan and Co., 1905.

Caraman, Philip, S. J. *Ignatius Loyola: A Biography of the Founder of the Jesuits*. San Francisco: Harper & Row, 1990.

Cavallini, Giuliana. *St. Martin de Porres: Apostle of Charity*. Translated by Caroline Holland. Rockford, Ill.: Tan Books & Publishers, Inc., 1979.

De Robeck, Nesta. *St. Clare of Assisi*. Milwaukee, Wis.: Bruce Publishing Company, 1951.

Derum, James Patrick. *The Porter of Saint Bonaventure's: The Life of Father Solanus Casey, Capuchin*. Detroit: Fidelity Press, 1968.

Dorcy, Mary Jean, O.P. *Saint Dominic*. Rockford, Ill.: Tan Books & Publishers, 1982.

Du Boulay, Shirley. *Teresa of Avila: Her Story*. Ann Arbor, Mich.: Servant Publications, 1995.

Fremantle, Anne. *Saints Alive!: The Lives of Thirteen Heroic Saints.* Garden City, N.Y.: Doubleday, 1978.

St. Gertrude. *The Life and Revelations of St. Gertrude.* Westminster, Md.: Christian Classics, 1987.

Ghéon, Henri. *St. Vincent Ferrer.* Translated by F. J. Sheed. New York: Sheed & Ward, 1939.

Ghezzi, Bert. *Voices of the Saints: A Year of Readings.* New York: Doubleday, 2000.

Healy, John. *The Life and Writings of St. Patrick.* Dublin: M. H. Gill & Son, 1905.

St. Ignatius of Loyola. *St. Ignatius' Own Story: As Told to Luis Gonzalez de Camara.* Translated by William J. Young, S.J. Chicago: Loyola University Press, 1980.

Kantor, Marvin. *The Origins of Christianity in Bohemia: Sources and Commentary.* Evanston, Ill.: Northwestern University Press, 1990.

Kearns, J. C., O.P. *The Life of Blessed Martín de Porres: Saintly American Negro and Patron of Social Justice.* New York: P. J. Kenedy & Sons, 1937.

Lappin, Peter. *Give Me Souls!: Life of Don Bosco.* Huntington, Ind.: Our Sunday Visitor, 1977.

Luce, Clare Boothe, ed. *Saints for Now.* New York: Sheed & Ward, 1952.

McGinley, Phyllis. *Saint-Watching.* New York: Viking Press, 1969.

Merton, Thomas. *What Are These Wounds?: The Life of a Cistercian Mystic, Saint Lutgarde of Aywières.* Milwaukee, Wis.: Bruce Publishing Company, 1950.

Montalembert, Count de. *The Life of Saint Elizabeth.* New York: P. J. Kenedy & Sons, n.d.

Musurillo, Herbert, ed. *The Acts of the Christian Martyrs.* Oxford: Clarendon Press, 1972.

Newcomb, James F. *St. Theresa Margaret of the Sacred Heart of Jesus.* New York: Benziger Brothers, 1934.

Purcell, Mary. *Don Francisco: The Story of St. Francis Xavier.* Westminster, Md.: Newman Press, 1954.

————. *Saint Anthony and His Times*. Garden City, N.Y.: Hanover House, 1960.

Raymond of Capua. *The Life of St. Catherine of Siena*. Translated by George Lamb. New York: P. J. Kenedy & Sons, 1960.

S. M. C. (Sister Mary Catherine). *Angel of the Judgment: A Life of Vincent Ferrer*. Notre Dame, Ind.: Ave Maria Press, 1954.

Sackville-West, V. *Saint Joan of Arc*. New York: The Literary Guild, 1936.

Sheed, F. J., ed. *Saints Are Not Sad: Forty Biographical Portraits*. New York: Sheed & Ward, 1949.

Simi, Gino J., and Mario M. Segreti. *Saint Francis of Paola: God's Miracle Worker Supreme*. Rockford, Ill.: Tan Books & Publishers, Inc., 1977.

Tanquerey, Adolphe, S.S. *The Spiritual Life: A Treatise on Ascetical and Mystical Theology*. Tournai, Belgium: Desclée & Co., 1930.

St. Teresa of Avila. *The Life of Teresa of Jesus*. Translated and edited by E. Allison Peers. Garden City, N. Y.: Image Books, 1960.

Thomas of Celano. *St. Francis of Assisi: First and Second Life of St. Francis*. Translated by Placid Hermann, O.F.M. Chicago: Franciscan Herald Press, 1963.

Thurston, Herbert, S. J., and Donald Attwater, eds. *Butler's Lives of the Saints*. 4 vols. Westminster, Md.: Christian Classics, Inc., 1956.

Vicaire, M.-H., O.P. *Saint Dominic and His Times*. Translated by Kathleen Pond. New York: McGraw-Hill, 1964.

Ward, Maisie. *Saints Who Made History: The First Five Centuries*. New York: Sheed & Ward, 1959.

Watkin, E. I. *Neglected Saints*. New York: Sheed & Ward, 1955.

Woodward, Kenneth L. *Making Saints*. New York: Touchstone Books, 1996.

Glossary

abbot: a man who is the head of an abbey of monks.

Albigensians: a religious sect based in southern France during the late twelfth and early thirteenth centuries that taught a dualism, affirming two eternal principles of good and evil.

Arianism: a heresy based on the teachings of Arius, an Alexandrian priest, who held that Christ was not truly God and that the Son was a creature and capable of sin. Condemned at the Council of Nicea in 325 and at the Council of Constantinople in 381.

Augustinian: member of an order that follows the monastic rule of St. Augustine.

Avignon papacy: period from 1309 to 1377 during which the popes, under the powerful influence of the French kings, resided in the southern French city of Avignon. The rest of Europe regarded the popes as the tools of France and described the situation as the "Babylonian captivity" of the papacy.

Benedictine Rule: a pattern of life developed in 540 by St. Benedict of Nursia for his monks and used by numerous religious commu nities of men and women throughout the Middle Ages.

Blessed: a title applied to a person whom the Roman Catholic Church allows to be recognized as worthy of being imitated.

canon: a member of a clerical group living according to a canon, or rule; a clergyman serving in a cathedral or collegiate church.

Capuchins: offshoot of the Friars Minor; founded in 1552 in an effort to return to the primitive simplicity of the order.

Carmelite order: the Order of Our Lady of Mount Carmel, founded in the twelfth century in Palestine; Carmelite communi ties of men and women spread throughout Europe in the thirteenth and fourteenth centuries.

catechist: a person who instructs others in Christian doctrine.

catechumen: a person who is receiving instruction in basic Christianity in preparation for baptism.

Cathari (Cathars): a dualist sect that was prominent in twelfth-century Germany; its adherents in France and Italy were called Albigenses or Albigensians.

chapter: an assembly or meeting of the canons of a cathedral.

Cîteaux: the central house of the Cistercian order, a strict Benedictine monastic community founded in the eleventh century.

Council of Trent: the nineteenth Ecumenical Council (1545–1563), called as a response to Protestantism and to the great need for moral and administrative reforms in the church.

diocese: the district under a bishop's supervision.

doctor of the church: a title given to Christian theologians and influencers of outstanding merit and acknowledged saintliness.

Dominican: See **Friars Preachers.**

Eucharist: Mass, the Lord's Supper, or Holy Communion; the central act of Christian worship.

faculty, faculties: license by a church authority to perform a function or hold an ecclesial office.

fathers of the church: early Christian authors whose authority on doctrinal matters carried special weight.

Friars Minor: the religious community of men founded by St. Francis of Assisi in the thirteenth century.

Friars Preachers: the religious community of men founded by St. Dominic in the thirteenth century.

host: the consecrated bread of the Eucharist.

Lent: a penitential season observed in preparation for Easter.

Liturgy of the Hours: the public prayer of the church, consisting of psalms, hymns, and Scripture and arranged so that it covers the entire day at specified intervals; required of priests and religious men and women and open to the participation of all.

Mass: the official public worship of the Catholic Church, consisting of the Liturgy of the Word (the proclamation of Scripture) and the Liturgy of the Eucharist (the representation of Christ's sacrifice and communion).

mitre: a tall, ornamented cap with peaks in front and back that is worn by abbots, bishops, and popes as a sign of their office.

novice: a person who has not yet taken vows but holds probationary membership in a religious group.

novitiate: the training program for new members of religious orders.

order: a religious community of men or women who live according to a rule of life.

papacy: the term used for the government or office of the pope.

porter: the doorkeeper and greeter at a monastery.

prior: the second in command under an abbot in a monastery; the head of a priory, a subordinate unit of a monastery.

provincial: the governor of a province, a geographical unit of a religious order.

religious: a man or woman who belongs to a religious order.

religious order: a community of men or women who are committed to living according to a rule of life.

spiritual director: a pastor or counselor who governs the Christian life of another person.

stigmata: the reproduction of the wounds of Christ's passion in or on the human body.

tertiary: a member of a Third Order, an association of laymen or laywomen who pattern their lives on the rule of a religious community but who continue to live ordinary secular lives.

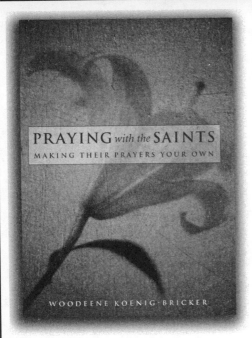